# *Life in the*
# THIRTEEN COLONIES

An Exact Prospect of CHARLESTOWN, the Metropolis of the Province of SOUTH CAROLINA.

# South Carolina

Richard Worth

**children's press®**
An imprint of
**SCHOLASTIC**

**Library of Congress Cataloging-in-Publication Data**

Worth, Richard.
 South Carolina / by Richard Worth.
  p. cm. — (Life in the thirteen colonies)
 Includes bibliographical references and index.
 ISBN 0–516–24579–1
 1. South Carolina—History—Colonial period, ca. 1600–1775—Juvenile literature. 2. South Carolina—
History—Revolution, 1775–1783—Juvenile literature. I. Title. II. Series.
 F272.W785 2004
 975.7'02—dc22

                2004002445

A Creative Media Applications Production
Design: Fabia Wargin Design
Editor: Laura Walsh
Copy Editor: Laurie Lieb
Proofreader: Tania Bissell
Content Research: Lauren Thogersen
Photo Researcher: Annette Cyr
Content Consultant: David Silverman, Ph.D.


Photo Credits © 2004

Cover: Upper left © North Wind Picture Archives; Upper right © Hulton Archive; Lower left © North Wind Picture Archives;
Lower right © Christie's Images/CORBIS; Background © North Wind Picture Archives; Title page © Hulton Archive; p. 2
© North Wind Picture Archives; p. 4 © North Wind Picture Archives; p. 6 © North Wind Picture Archives; p. 9 © North Wind
Picture Archives; p. 13 © North Wind Picture Archives; p. 14 © North Wind Picture Archives; p. 17 © North Wind Picture
Archives; p. 21 © ClipArt.com; p. 22 © Hulton Archive; p. 24 © Hulton Archive; p. 26 © North Wind Picture Archives; p. 27
© North Wind Picture Archives; p. 28 © North Wind Picture Archives; p. 30 © North Wind Picture Archives; p. 32 © North
Wind Picture Archives; p. 36 © North Wind Picture Archives; p. 41 © Hulton Archive; p. 42 © Hulton Archive; p. 47 © North
Wind Picture Archives; p. 50 © North Wind Picture Archives; p. 52 © North Wind Picture Archives; p. 57 © North Wind
Picture Archives; p. 60 © North Wind Picture Archives; p. 63 © Hulton Archive; p. 64-65 From left to right © Hulton Archive;
© Richard T. Nowitz/CORBIS; © The Colonial Williamsburg Foundation; © The Colonial Williamsburg Foundation; © The
Colonial Williamsburg Foundation; © The Colonial Williamsburg Foundation; © Todd A. Gipstein/CORBIS; © Lee Snider;
Lee Snider/CORBIS; © The Colonial Williamsburg Foundation; p. 66 Brooklyn Museum of Art, New York, USA/Gift of the
Brooklyn Institute of Arts and Sciences/Bridgeman Art Library; p. 70 © Richard T. Nowitz/CORBIS; p. 72 © Paul A.
Souders/CORBIS; p. 74 © North Wind Picture Archives; p. 76 © North Wind Picture Archives; p. 78 © North Wind Picture
Archives; p. 80 © North Carolina Museum of Art/CORBIS; p. 83 © North Wind Picture Archives; p. 84 © North Wind
Picture Archives; p. 89 © North Wind Picture Archives; p. 92 © North Wind Picture Archives; p. 94 © North Wind Picture
Archives; p. 99 © North Wind Picture Archives; p. 102 © Hulton Archive; p. 104 © Hulton Archive; p. 108© Peggy & Ronald
Barnett/CORBIS; p. 1113 © Hulton Archive; p. 115 © North Wind Picture Archives; p. 118-119 Background © North Wind
Picture Archives; From left to right © North Wind Picture Archives; © North Wind Picture Archives; © North Wind Picture
Archives; © North Wind Picture Archives; © Hulton Archive; © North Wind Picture Archives; © North Wind Picture
Archives; © North Wind Picture Archives

# CONTENTS

# THE ORIGINAL THIRTEEN COLONIES, 1775

NEW FRANCE

MAINE
*(part of Mass.)*

St. Lawrence River

Lake Champlain

NEW HAMPSHIRE

• Falmouth

Connecticut River

• Portsmouth
• Newburyport
Salem •
Boston •

NEW HAMPSHIRE

MASSACHUSETTS

Cape Cod

Lake Ontario

Mohawk R.

Albany •

NEW YORK

Hudson R.

Hartford •

• Newport

New Haven •

RHODE ISLAND
CONNECTICUT

Lake Erie

Delaware R.

Susquehanna R.

Long Island

New York •

Ohio River

Appalachian Mountains

Pittsburgh •

PENNSYLVANIA

York •

Philadelphia •

Perth Amboy •

• Burlington

NEW JERSEY

Baltimore •

• New Castle

DELAWARE

Potomac R.

MARYLAND

Alexandria •

Atlantic Ocean

James River

Richmond •

• Chesapeake Bay

• Williamsburg

VIRGINIA

• Norfolk

Roanoke River

Edenton •

Hillsboro •

Halifax •

Salem •

NORTH CAROLINA

Bath •

Cape Hatteras

Salisbury •

New Bern •

Pamlico Sound

• Charlotte

Cross Creek

Cape Fear R.

Camden •

Wilmington •

SOUTH CAROLINA

• Georgetown

Augusta •

Savannah River

GEORGIA

• Charles Town

Savannah •

SPANISH TERRITORY

NORTH
EAST
WEST
SOUTH

## Legend
— Colonial boundaries
(The western boundaries of many colonies were undefined in 1775).

0    125    250

Scale in Miles

# A Nation Grows
## From Thirteen Colonies

South Carolina lies in the southeastern region of the United States. The Atlantic Ocean forms its eastern border. North Carolina lies to the north and Georgia to the south. It was one of the original thirteen colonies. The first explorers who came to South Carolina found a land of forests, rivers, and swamps filled with wildlife. The climate was hot and humid. There was also much fertile farmland.

Four groups of people shaped the story of the South Carolina colony. Indian peoples had lived in this land for thousands of years. Rich European farmers came to build large plantations. Slaves were forced to work for the plantation owners. And simple backcountry farmers came to seek freedom and opportunity. This is the story of how these four groups lived, fought, worked, played, and finally made South Carolina part of the United States.

*The map shows the thirteen English colonies in 1775. The colored sections show the areas that were settled at that time.*

# CHAPTER ONE

# European Explorers

## The Spanish Arrive

In October 1492, three Spanish sailing ships bobbed up and down on the windswept waters of the Caribbean Sea. The ships bore a blood-red cross on their sails. This was the symbol of Spain.

All three of the ships were less than 60 feet (18 meters) long—about the size of four minivans end-to-end. Yet they had sailed more than 2,000 miles (3,200 kilometers) across the Atlantic Ocean. The expedition was commanded by an Italian explorer named Christopher Columbus. He was sent by Spain's King Ferdinand and Queen Isabella. Admiral Columbus had convinced the Spanish rulers that he could find a new route to the riches of China by sailing west.

*This drawing from Columbus's time shows him exploring the New World.*

Until then, the only way to reach China was to travel thousands of miles by land across Asia, or sail around the southern tip of Africa. Either way, the journey took more than a year and was very dangerous. Columbus never did reach China. What he found instead was America.

Over the next three decades, the Spanish explored this New World. They claimed vast territories in the Caribbean, Central America, and South America. They also explored and claimed lands on the North American continent, including parts of what is now South Carolina.

*The spiritual leader of the Indians in the Carolina region was called a shaman.*

Columbus sent reports about his discovery back to Spain. He told stories of the gold necklaces and nose rings worn by Native Americans. The desire for gold swept through Spain. Soon Spanish explorers and settlers were making the dangerous voyage to the New World in search of gold and other riches.

The Spanish started their search for riches on the islands of the Caribbean and in Mexico. In each of these areas they found thriving civilizations of Native peoples. At first many of these Native people thought the Spanish were friends. But Columbus and other Spanish explorers regarded the Indians as savages.

They enslaved them and forced them to work on Spanish farms and in mines. Worse, the Spanish exposed the Indians to diseases such as measles and smallpox. The Indians had no natural defenses against these diseases. Thousands of Indian people died.

# The Search for Slaves

Soon, the Spanish began to run out of Indian slaves and looked for new places to find more workers. In 1520, the Spanish sent a ship from the Caribbean to North America in search of slaves. The Spanish ship was commanded by Francisco Gordillo.

In June 1521, Gordillo landed on the coast of present-day South Carolina, probably near Winyah Bay. He named the area *Carolana*, in honor of Charles V, the current Spanish king. In Latin, Carolana means "land of Charles." Gordillo claimed the land for his king and the country of Spain. This new territory included what later became the colonies of South Carolina, North Carolina, and Georgia.

When they landed, the Spanish explorers were greeted at the shore by one of the Indian tribes that lived along the Carolana coast. The Indians were called the Chicora. They had never seen white men before and thought the strangers were "great monsters or gods." Gordillo pretended to make friends with the Chicora. He promised them beads and other presents if they came on board his ship. The Chicora fell into the trap. Once the Indians were on board, the Spanish sailors chained them up and sailed for the Caribbean, taking their captives with them. The Indians had never been so far from home. They feared that they would live the rest of their lives in slavery. Several of the captives were so distressed that they refused to eat and died of starvation during the voyage.

*Spanish explorers enslaved and mistreated the Indians they met in America.*

# The First Settlement

One of the Indians who survived would eventually outwit his Spanish captors. The Spanish named him Francisco de Chicora, after the name of his tribe. His true Indian name was never recorded.

De Chicora quickly learned to speak Spanish. Then he spun a wondrous story about huge deposits of gold and vast fields of corn in his native land. Francisco de Chicora had probably never seen either of these things. He was just trying to trick the Spanish in order to return home. But a Spanish judge, Lucas Vázquez de Ayllón, was convinced by what he heard. In 1526, Ayllón led a large expedition of several ships and over 500 settlers to the Carolana coast in search of riches. Ayllón brought Francisco de Chicora along as a guide and interpreter.

Bad luck followed Ayllón's expedition from the beginning. Before landing in Carolana, one of the ships sank with all its supplies. When the remaining ships landed along the Carolana coast, the Spanish found a dense wilderness. Francisco de Chicora seized his opportunity. He slipped away with other Indian slaves and was never seen again. Ayllón was left in an uncharted land with no maps or guide. But he was hungry for gold and began to march inland.

Unlike the Indians of the region, the Spanish were not skilled at moving through the dense woods that grew along Carolana's coasts and rivers. Ayllón's expedition made slow progress trudging through the swamps and woods. There were no roads or trails and no one to guide them. The Spanish explorers wore heavy clothing, leather boots, and armor that made them uncomfortable in the heat and humidity. But Ayllón would not give up.

Finally, the Spanish built a small settlement along a river. It was the first European town in South Carolina. Unfortunately, they did not realize that the swampy riverbank was filled with disease-carrying mosquitoes. Sickness swept through the new village. Over 300 settlers died, including Ayllón himself. This was too much for the remaining Spanish colonists. After only a few months, they abandoned their settlement and returned to the Spanish colonies in the Caribbean.

# Indian People

Although life was difficult for the Spanish newcomers to South Carolina, Indian tribes had thrived there for several thousand years. They established villages, grew crops, made pottery, and created successful governments. Their farms produced large crops year after year.

More than two dozen tribes lived in the territory that the Spaniards named Carolana. Along the Atlantic coast, near present-day Pawley's Island, lived the small Chicora tribe. They had been the first Native Americans to encounter the Spanish in 1521. In the southern part of Carolana lived other small tribes called the Stono, Wando, Westo, and Kiawah. In addition, large tribes, such as the Cherokee, Yamasee, and Catawba, flourished in the area.

# The Cherokee

Away from the coast, in the mountains of western Carolana, lived the Cherokee. They were the largest and most powerful Indian tribe in the region. By the sixteenth century, about 200 Cherokee villages dotted the region. Each village contained thirty to sixty houses called wigwams. Extended families made up of parents, grand-parents, and children shared the same home. In winter, families lived in circular houses built of branches and mud. Although these houses were sometimes crowded, each person had his or her own place.

*Indian woman from about 1585.*

## Women's Work

The Cherokee were shocked when they later saw European men farming and tending livestock. They never understood why male settlers did so much women's work.

9

In each house, there was a common area where the family ate with a fire to cook food and keep the family warm. In the summer, the Cherokee moved to more open, rectangular houses. Openings in the walls allowed breezes to cool the inside, helping Cherokee families withstand Carolana's hot and humid summer months.

At the center of each village was a large council house. A sacred fire burned inside. The council house had seven sides. The sides symbolized the seven clans, or groups, of the Cherokee people: the Bird, Paint, Deer, Wolf, Blue, Long Hair, and Wild Potato clans. The Indians met in the council house to make important decisions and hold religious festivals. In November of each year, the council house filled with villagers celebrating the New Year's Dance. At this festival, they lit a new sacred fire, which was kept burning until the following New Year.

# Cherokee Life

Work was divided equally among the men and women of the Cherokee tribe. Women did the farming. They planted the seeds, tended the crops, and then harvested them. There was little time for them to leave the fields to care for their babies, so they worked in the fields with newly born children strapped to their backs in cradleboards. Cradleboards were made of wood with curved sides. They had leather straps strung over them to tie the baby firmly in place. Older children helped their mothers farm and tended to other chores such as gathering firewood for the village.

Women played other important roles in the tribe. The Cherokee in each clan were related through their mothers. So a man could not marry within his clan. Children belonged to their mother's clan, not their father's. Women also participated in the decisions made by the tribe at the council house. These decisions guided the two Cherokee chiefs, the Peace Chief and the War Chief.

## The Three Sisters

The Cherokee were experienced and successful farmers. Each Cherokee village was surrounded by fields of corn, squash, and beans. These crops were known by Indians as the Three Sisters. The Three Sisters demonstrated the Cherokee's knowledge of the land. The three crops were planted together in a small mound. Beans supplied nitrogen, a rich fertilizer, to the soil. This made the other two plants grow stronger. The beans, which were climbing plants, grew up around the cornstalks, using them for support. The squash leaves kept the soil moist and reduced the number of weeds.

Cherokee men did the hunting. They made arrows from reeds and wooden bows to hunt deer and other animals. They also trapped and caught fish in the many rivers and streams that flowed through the Carolana woodlands.

## Lacrosse

A favorite game shared by Indians in the Carolana region was stickball. In this game, players used long sticks with deerskin pouches to carry a leather ball and shoot it through wooden goalposts. French trappers who observed the game called it lacrosse because the stick reminded them of a Christian cross. Lacrosse is played today at many colleges. Unlike today's game, which has a sixty-minute time limit, the game played by Indians often ranged over miles of woodland and lasted for days. Some Indian tribes used the game to settle disputes instead of going to war. Needless to say, stickball was a very rough game.

When a deer was killed, every part of the animal was used by the tribe. The meat was cooked and eaten, or dried so it could be stored and then eaten during the winter. The deerskin was made into clothing. Women removed the hair from the skin and soaked the skin in a mixture made of water and animal brains to soften it. Then the skin was stretched and dried on racks outside the houses. Finally, it was cut with stone knives and sewn into clothing and moccasins. The deer's bones and antlers were carved into combs, needles, and other useful tools.

Like the Cherokee, the other Indian tribes of Carolana developed complex, thriving cultures. They grew the Three Sisters and hunted and fished in Carolana's woods and along the Atlantic coast. They lived in balance with the land and maintained stable governments for centuries before the arrival of Spanish and other European explorers. Their way of life would change dramatically beginning in the sixteenth century as the Spanish, French, and English discovered the rich land that Carolana offered.

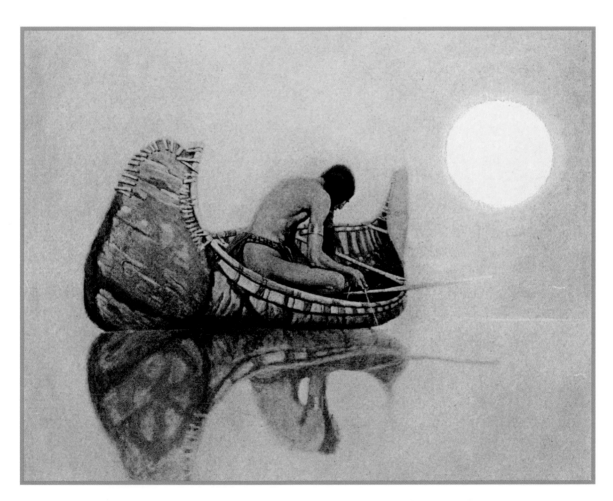

*Indians fished from canoes and along the banks of Carolana's many rivers, lakes, and estuaries.*

# The Spanish Return

In 1539 the Spanish returned to Carolana, more than a decade after Ayllón's unsuccessful attempt to establish a settlement. This time, the Spanish had only one goal, to find gold and silver. A Spanish military expedition landed south of Carolana in present-day Florida. It was led by a conquistador, or Spanish soldier, named Hernando de Soto. De Soto's soldiers marched north into Carolana. They hacked pathways through the uncharted swamps and forests with their swords.

*When the Spanish soldier de Soto first arrived in Carolana, he was met as a friend by the local Indians.*

Along the way, the Spaniards met Indian peoples, including the Cherokee. One of de Soto's conquistadors wrote that the "country was well inhabited, producing much corn." He added that the soldiers pursued and killed some Indians they encountered. "Two were discovered engaged in picking beans, and might have escaped, but a woman being present, the wife of one of them, they stood to fight." Their bows and arrows were no match for Spanish guns and swords. Others in nearby villages were enslaved by de Soto and his men.

De Soto found no gold or silver in Carolana and soon led his men westward toward the Mississippi River. However, the Spanish soldiers left something terrible behind. They exposed the Carolana Indians to diseases they brought from Europe. Thousands of Cherokee and other Native Americans died. Seventy-five percent of the Cherokee population was killed by smallpox and other European diseases brought by de Soto's army.

Although the Spanish did not find the riches they were searching for in Carolana, they continued to explore the area and claimed it for the Spanish king. The cruel actions of Spanish explorers such as de Soto caused the Indians to mistrust the Spanish and fight against Spanish settlements. This resistance would eventually drive the Spanish from Carolana.

# The French Arrive

The Spanish were not the only explorers to set their sights on the New World. In 1562, a French expedition led by Jean Ribault reached the North American coast. He sailed into a bay that he named Port Royal. Ribault called it "one of the greatest and fayrest havens in the world." He and his men built a small settlement they called Charlesfort, after their king, Charles IX.

Ribault left some of his men at the fort and sailed back to France to get additional supplies. Before he could return, the settlers ran short of food. To make matters worse, they were attacked by Indians who thought the French were stealing their land. The French settlers were afraid they would be killed or starve to death. They quickly built a ship, loaded it with the small amount of food they had left, and sailed for France. The voyage was long and their supplies ran out. The settlers ate everything they could, including their shoes. By the time they were rescued by a passing English ship, the crew had resorted to cannibalism, killing and eating their shipmates.

The French were through with trying to settle Carolana. By 1586, the Spanish left Carolana for good and retreated to their settlements in the Caribbean and Florida. The combination of Indian resistance and the difficult environment was too much for settlers from both countries. Soon, new invaders from Europe would discover the potential riches of Carolana. These colonists would prove too powerful for the Indians and they would find ways to overcome the challenges of Carolana's environment.

*Colonial settlers needed many skills. The French colonists left behind by Ribault built a ship using wood and other materials they obtained from the Carolana countryside.*

# CHAPTER TWO

# An English Colony

## The English Invasion

While the Spanish were exploring Carolana, another European country was busy claiming territory elsewhere in the New World. Spain's old enemy, England, had established successful colonies in the northeastern part of America and as far south as Virginia. During the early 1600s, the English turned their attention to the territory south of Virginia. Unlike the Spanish, English settlers would establish a thriving colony in Carolana.

In 1663, King Charles II of England claimed the Spanish territory of Carolana for England. He changed the name slightly, to Carolina. The English king wanted the money the new territory could bring but he wanted someone else to run it for him. So he gave eight of his most important subjects the right to develop Carolina for England. The eight Englishmen were called proprietors.

*This map shows how South Carolina looked about 1775.*

The proprietors were given all "Rights, Jurisdictions, Privileges, Prerogatives, Royalties, Liberties…and Franchises of what kind soever within the Country." This meant that they could make laws with the advice of a legislature, raise an army to fight enemies, and run a court system. In short, they owned the new Carolina territory. The proprietors hoped to make money by selling or renting land to settlers. Not one of the proprietors ever visited Carolina.

## Early Explorations

The Carolina territory was enormous. It filled over one-third of the present-day United States. It stretched from Virginia southward to Florida, and from the Atlantic coast westward all the way to the Pacific Ocean. At the time, no Englishman had explored this vast territory. But that did not stop the English from claiming the land for their country.

Before they could send settlers, the proprietors had to know more about the country. In 1663, they sent an expedition led by Captain William Hilton to explore the Carolina coast. Hilton sailed south to Port Royal and explored the rivers in the area. He found what the proprietors had hoped for, "good tracts of land, dry, well wooded, pleasant and delightful as we have seen any where in the world." He raved about the abundant wildlife in the area, including deer, turkeys, wolves, and ducks. He also described the variety of trees, such as oak, maple, walnut, birch, and beech, as well as pines, "tall and good for boards or masts" for ships. In addition, Hilton said that the Indians had planted fields with corn with "as large Cornstalks or bigger, than we have seen any where else."

In 1666, another English expedition sailed to Carolina. This voyage was led by Captain Robert Sandford. Sandford visited Port Royal, which he praised as a good place for a settlement with room for "habitations for thousands of people" and their animals. The local [cacique] was so impressed with Sandford that he brought his nephew on board the captain's ship. He pleaded with Sandford to take the boy with

*This engraving from the mid-1700s of Ostenaco (also known as Outacite) shows how a Cherokee cacique might have looked. His name means "Man Killer."*

him so he could see the houses where the English lived, eat their food, and learn their language. In return, one member of the English expedition, Dr. Henry Woodward, decided to stay behind to live with the Indians and learn their ways.

The explorers' descriptions made the new land sound like paradise. They were written up and printed as advertisements to lure the English to Carolina. Many people in England were poor. The proprietors offered them land at low rents and a new, more successful life. All they had to do was leave their homeland and sail 2,000 miles (3,200 kilometers) across the Atlantic Ocean to an uncharted wilderness. Many people thought this was a fair deal. As time passed, more settlers came to Carolina. The next step was to decide what the government of the new colony would be like.

New and Accurate ACCOUNT

OF THE

PROVINCES

OF

SOUTH-CAROLINA

AND

GEORGIA:

With many curious and useful Observations on the Trade, Navigation and Plantations of *Great-Britain*, compared with her most powerful maritime Neighbours in antient and modern Times.

*Pamphlets such as this were published in England to try to convince settlers to come to Carolina.*

## Preparing the First Settlement

The proprietors wrote a description of how the new colony should be governed. It was called the Fundamental Constitutions of Carolina. The Fundamental Constitutions called for a governor and an elected assembly to run the colonial government. The governor would live in Carolina and advise the proprietors. Members of the assembly needed to own at least 500 acres (200 hectares) of land.

The Fundamental Constitutions did something very unusual for the time. It gave settlers religious freedom. In many countries of Europe during the seventeenth century, people were not permitted to practice their religion. In Spain, for example, Catholicism was the only religion permitted by the government. Jews were forced to leave the country. In France, the Catholic king drove out Protestant groups called Huguenots.

The fact that religious freedom was permitted in Carolina was very attractive to many settlers from Europe. Making religious freedom an important feature of the Fundamental Constitutions insured that there would be a steady stream of settlers to Carolina.

When it was time to send settlers to the new colony, the proprietors assembled a fleet of three ships with about a hundred settlers. In 1669, they sailed from England, stopping at the island of Bermuda to pick up William Sayle, who would be Carolina's first governor.

In March 1670, the expedition went ashore near Port Royal. They were met by a group of friendly Indians wearing deerskins.

The governor met with the Indian cacique, who warned him that the area around Port Royal was not a good place to put a settlement. Another tribe, the Westos, had recently raided the area and might come back. Port Royal was also close to settlements in Florida where the Spanish still had troops. Spain wanted to keep the English out of the area. So the Spanish might persuade Indian tribes to attack a new English settlement.

The settlers took the chief's advice and sailed northward to the Kiawah River. It looked like the perfect place to build a town. They renamed the river the Ashley and built the settlement of Charles Town.

At first, Charles Town was little more than a few cabins and a crude dock. As time passed, the new town prospered. Its location was ideal for ships to sail to and for goods to be transported downriver. Charles Town quickly became the center of the colony's economic and social life.

*By 1673, the settlement of Charles Town along the Ashley River was already a bustling community of farmers and traders.*

# Tough Life

Carolina was an uncomfortable and sometimes dangerous place for the new settlers. There were dangerous animals, including alligators and poisonous snakes, to deal with. Trees had to be cleared, cabins built, and fields planted in order for the colony to survive. Before the colonists could harvest their first crop, food began to run out. Governor Sayle sent a ship north to Virginia, an English colony where there had been permanent settlements since 1607. The ship returned with supplies, including pigs and cows. The colony was off to a successful start. Soon more settlers arrived.

The thick forests that had made life difficult for the Spanish were also a problem for the new English farmers. Clearing the land of trees was a difficult job. Settlers could clear only one or two acres of land per year. By the time he died, a farmer may have been able to clear 100 acres (40 hectares). That was barely enough land for a small farm. Many of the trees that grew in the Carolina forest were hundreds of years old, with trunks up to 6 feet (1.8 meters) thick. Cutting these trees with an ax and saw was nearly impossible for the new settlers. Instead, they cut a band or "girdle" around the tree trunks with an ax. This caused the trees to die. After a year or more, when the trees were dead and dried out, the settlers set fire to them to clear the land.

However, a farmer was likely to have to plow around large tree stumps for many years to come.

Settlers had to do everything by themselves. They had to gather wood from surrounding forests to build a fire. They also had to cut trees to build houses. Wood was used to make farm implements, too, including hoes, shovels, and ploughs. With their tools, farmers planted corn, the main source of food for most families. As one historian wrote:

*Settlers cleared the land for farms by cutting trees. They used horses to pull their plows and oxen to haul away tree stumps.*

"No part of the [corn] plant went unused: the stalks served as winter fodder for cattle, the husks to stuff mattresses, the cobs as…tool handles, and the bowls of corncob pipes." Families worked together to plant corn in the spring and then to harvest it in the fall. There were no markets or stores to buy food or other supplies. If a family did not produce enough to eat, they starved.

## A Hard Life

Settlers in Carolina generally lived in families made up of parents and children. Families were almost self-sufficient. Everyone worked on the family farm, from the youngest to the oldest. The workday began at sunup and ended at sundown. During summer, this could be fourteen to sixteen hours. Children began doing chores at the age of two or three. In addition to farm skills, children learned religious values and possibly a little reading and writing from their parents. If a mother or father died from an accident or disease such as smallpox or

*This young farm girl helps her mother prepare the family meal by peeling apples.*

malaria, the children often went to live with relatives. However, many orphans were forced to become servants to other families who would take them in.

# A Growing Colony

Over the next few years, the colonists planted crops and traded furs with the Indians near Charles Town. The settlement on the Ashley River had one big drawback: the river flooded periodically, washing out houses and sometimes drowning settlers. The colonists found a better place for their town on a peninsula between the Ashley and the

*These backcountry settlers used a plumping mill to grind corn into cornmeal.*

Cooper rivers. They moved to this new location in 1680. It became the permanent settlement of Charles Town and eventually grew into the present-day city of Charleston, South Carolina.

By 1680, about 1,000 colonists lived in Carolina. They supported themselves primarily by farming and trading. However, the local Indians had become upset with the practices of the traders. They believed that the traders were dishonest men who tried to trick the Indians by not paying enough for the deerskins. The Indians were also angered by the settlers who captured Indian men and women and sold them into slavery.

These problems would continue as the colony grew and the Indians realized that their way of life was threatened. Carolina would also face other challenges as the colonists established new settlements, fought off pirates, and eventually changed the structure of its colonial government.

# CHAPTER THREE

# The Colony Grows

## Backcountry Newcomers

By 1700, Carolina was missing only one ingredient to make it a successful colony. It needed more people. The proprietors wanted to send as many settlers as possible to the colony. Because the proprietors had set up the Fundamental Constitutions, settlers from many religious groups came to the colony. Carolina offered these groups a place to live and worship as they chose.

In 1683, the proprietors persuaded a group of 150 Protestants from Scotland to make the dangerous voyage to America and settle in Carolina. The new settlers built a town near Port Royal. They called their village Stuart Town. The new settlement survived only a short time but it was an important starting point for the new settlers. Within three years, Spanish soldiers marched north from Florida and destroyed the new town. They regarded the Scottish settlement as a

*A Carolina backcountry settler pours water into a bucket from her well. There was no indoor plumbing in the Carolina backcountry.*

31

threat to Florida, just as the Indian cacique had warned years before. The Scottish settlers fled, but they did not leave Carolina. Many of them moved west and set up farms.

Like the Scots, other Protestant groups came to Carolina looking for the religious freedoms promised in Carolina's Fundamental Constitutions. These groups included Huguenots from France and Baptists and Presbyterians from other European countries. Most of these newcomers moved to the area west and south of Charles Town, called the backcountry. They established farms and villages. They grew crops and traded with the merchants in Charles Town. As the new colony grew, these backcountry settlers became an important force in Carolina.

*Governor John Archdale met with Carolina's settlers to discuss the colony's government.*

As the number of colonists increased, the Carolina assembly grew more important. When a new governor named John Archdale arrived, settlers from all parts of the colony met with him. They convinced the governor that no laws should be changed without the consent of the assembly. This was an important step toward democracy. The assembly used this new democratic power during the next decades to achieve greater independence from England.

# Facing Disaster

The population of Charles Town grew from about 1,100 settlers in 1690 to about 2,000 in 1700. Farmers and others came to Carolina seeking a new life. The new settlers overcame many challenges as Charles Town faced fire, floods, and disease. In 1698, the city was devastated by a terrible fire that destroyed nearly half its houses. As a result, the assembly passed a new law that required homeowners to build their chimneys of brick or stone instead of wood.

## Southern Houses

Before 1700, most Carolina houses were small, one-room structures. The entire family lived, ate, and slept in a room about the size of the average living room today. A stone fireplace located at one end heated the house, provided most of the light, and was used to cook the meals. There was no bathroom or running water. Buckets were used to carry water from a stream or well into the house. Windows were small and often made of greased paper instead of expensive and fragile glass.

Settlers slept on straw mats since beds were expensive and bulky. Most other furniture was handmade.

As time passed, homes became larger and more comfortable. Settlers added rooms and bought furniture. The dirt floor was often replaced with bricks or wooden planks. Candles and oil lamps gave additional light. Even with these improvements, settlers' homes were much simpler than the typical house today.

As the townspeople rebuilt from the ashes of the 1698 fire, a powerful hurricane struck. More homes were destroyed and people were drowned. Then, a terrible outbreak of smallpox ravaged the city. Governor Archdale wrote in a letter, "We have had the small pox amongst us nine or ten months which hath been very infectious and mortal. We have lost by the distemper 200 or 300 persons." This was an enormous number of people in a population of only 2,000.

## Deadly Disease

Diseases like smallpox were often brought by ships coming into Charles Town harbor. Beginning in 1698, no ship could land if any of the sailors on board were sick. However, laws alone could not protect Charles Town from disease. In 1699, the city was struck by yellow fever. Many people became deathly ill. They had high fevers and vomited blood. In the final stages of the disease, their skin turned a yellowish color. There was no cure for yellow fever. Victims often died in less than a week. An average of five people died every day in Charles Town until the epidemic ran its course.

Charles Town had a serious problem with its location. The city was built on swamps and wetlands that were breeding grounds for mosquitoes that carried the deadly yellow fever virus. The town would suffer from outbreaks of the disease throughout its history.

# Progress

Settlers and townspeople knew that their lives could end tragically without warning from disease or natural disasters. In spite of these dangers, hardy new settlers continued to come to Carolina in search of land and religious freedom. Tough times did not stop progress in Charles Town. In 1698, the assembly established a public library. The small city also had a post office. Settlers could send letters to the Caribbean islands and to Europe. However, there were no schools in Charles Town, so many settlers received no education and could not read or write.

## Apprenticeships

Many boys left home to become apprentices at the age of about twelve. Apprentices learned to become butchers, bakers, carpenters, coopers (barrel makers), and other trades by working for skilled tradesmen called masters. During his apprenticeship, the boy often lived in the master's shop for seven years in exchange for his training. The conditions were often harsh and demanding.

Afterward, the young man could open his own shop or work for another tradesman for wages. Apprenticeships were only for boys. Girls remained at home with their parents until they married, often in their teens. At home they learned the skills they would need to maintain a household. They learned to cook, sew, tend gardens, and raise their younger brothers and sisters.

In spite of natural disasters and bouts of disease, Charles Town harbor was one of the busiest ports in America. Ships from England and the Caribbean carried on a lively trade with the colony. From the port, Carolina merchants shipped a variety of products to other countries. Ships were loaded with beef and pork raised on farms surrounding Charles Town. Sap from the many pine trees in the Carolina forests was made into tar and pitch. These black, sticky substances were used to seal the boards and planks of wooden ships. They were packed into barrels manufactured from Carolina trees. There was a great demand for these products in England because of the huge number of warships and trading vessels in the English fleet. Charles Town grew prosperous as the seventeenth century came to a close.

*Slaves worked in the hot, humid Carolina rice fields while the overseer watched from horseback.*

# Seeds of Slavery

As Carolina grew, no one could predict that a tiny grain would change the face of the colony. Until about 1700, Charles Town was surrounded by small farms. The discovery of a new crop caused these farms to grow into large plantations. The crop was rice. Rice plants thrived in the hot, wet Carolina climate. The riverbanks and tidal regions around Charles Town were ideal for growing this grain because rice fields must be flooded. By the early 1720s, over 1 million acres (405,000 hectares) of Carolina farmland were planted with rice. It became the colony's leading export to Europe and the Caribbean and would become Carolina's most profitable crop.

Growing rice promised great wealth for Carolina farmers. However, rice plantations required very intense and often backbreaking work. Land had to be cleared. Many acres had to be planted in spring. The rice fields required constant weeding and tending. In the fall, the crop had to be harvested and the rice grains separated from the rest of the plant. Plantation owners needed thousands of inexpensive workers to grow the huge quantity of rice they could sell to European markets. In the eighteenth century, cheap labor meant slaves.

In about 1740, South Carolina plantations began to grow indigo. Indigo is a plant from which blue dye was made.

Indigo-dyed clothing was highly prized by the wealthy aristocrats of England. Royal blue, the color used for the robes of kings and queens, was produced from indigo dye. Like rice, growing and harvesting indigo required grueling, intense work. Indigo plantations also needed many slaves. The slaves spent long hours under the hot sun, often battling swarms of flies and mosquitoes as well as poisonous snakes while they worked in the indigo fields. The introduction of this new crop brought huge profits to plantation owners. Together, rice and indigo ensured that slavery would be part of life in Carolina for more than a hundred years.

## The Indigo Experiment

The first South Carolina planter to successfully grow indigo was a woman, Elizabeth Lucas. Elizabeth's father was an officer in the British army who owned a large estate. In 1740, Major George Lucas was called away from his plantation to serve in a war with Spain. He left Elizabeth in charge of his plantation at Wappoo Creek. There she began experimenting with indigo seed that her father had purchased in the Caribbean. Her experiment was so successful that indigo became one of South Carolina's most profitable crops.

# Carolina Slaves

As the rice and indigo plantations around Charles Town grew, so did the number of slaves needed to work in the fields. Slaves had been a part of Carolina's history from the earliest settlements. In fact, the colony was first established by the Spanish in search of slaves.

Slaves did most of the work on large plantations and farms, but plantation owners were not the only ones to own slaves. Many small farmers and tradesmen owned one or two slaves as well. Some slaves were put to work herding cattle. Still others went to work in Charles Town helping artisans, such as carpenters and blacksmiths. Slaves often worked side by side with their masters. According to one observer at the time, as new settlers established their homesteads, they "cutt down a few Trees, to split…Clapboards and therewith make small Houses or Huts to shelter the slaves."

About 15 percent of Carolina's total population in 1708 were Indian slaves. Settlers captured Indian slaves with the help of other Indian tribes. Slave hunting parties would travel many miles through the forests until they reached an Indian village. Then they launched a surprise attack, killing any Indians who put up a fight. The rest of the villagers—men, women, and children—were captured and sold into slavery. In the early eighteenth century, a slave trader named Thomas Nairne went on a raid with the Yamasee tribe to

Florida. He explained that his party traveled in their canoes along "large inland lakes, some of them joined together…to go a Slave Catching." They captured over thirty slaves before being attacked by a band of Indians who used harpoons "made of Iron and Fish bones." But the Yamasee defeated their attackers and brought the slaves back to Carolina. As Nairne put it, "we the Indians and colonists have…been entirely knifing all the Indian towns in Florida." Nairne was eventually burned at the stake by the Yamasee because he was competing with them for Indian slaves.

Although Indians were often captured and put to work on Carolina plantations, by far the largest source of slaves for the colony was Africa. In fact, by 1708, African slaves outnumbered whites in the colony. African slaves were shipped to North America by European slave traders who worked along the coast of Africa. They bartered for slaves with tribes who captured other Africans and sold them to the Europeans. These slaves were brutally torn away from their villages, roped together, and forced to travel hundreds of miles to the coast. There they were exchanged for beads, pots, knives, and guns.

The traders branded the slaves with marks representing their trading companies. The marks were burned into the slaves' skin with red-hot branding irons. Large groups of slaves were then chained together and held in pens along the beach like cattle. Eventually, they were sent to America on filthy, crowded ships. The horrible trip across the Atlantic Ocean from Africa to North America was known as the Middle Passage. The conditions on the slave ships were so cramped that the people could barely move. Many contracted diseases, such as malaria or yellow fever, and thousands died. When they reached Carolina, the slaves were unloaded in Charles Town and sold to the colonists at auctions.

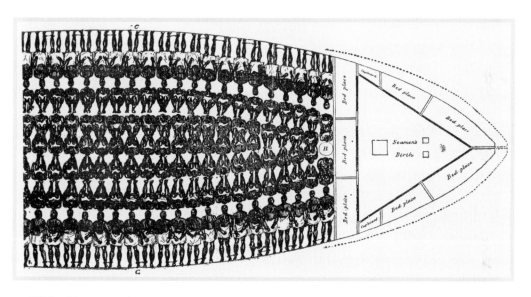

*This diagram from 1750 shows how tightly slaves were packed into slave ships bound for America. There was almost no room to move in the dark, damp hold of the slave ship.*

The number of slaves in Carolina grew rapidly. Small farms surrounding Charles Town expanded into large plantations. Soon, the economy of the colony depended upon slave labor. Although many white settlers became prosperous, the majority of people in Carolina lived in poverty as slaves.

# The Middle Passage

Olaudah Equiano and his sister were captured by slave traders in Africa during the eighteenth century. Eventually the two children were separated and, except for one brief occasion, never saw each other again. Equiano was taken to the west coast of Africa and loaded onto a slave ship. He was taken below deck, where, he explained, "I received such a salutation in my nostrils as I had never experienced in my life: so that with the loathsomeness of the stench [from the bodies of the other slaves and their wastes] I became so sick and low that I was not able to eat, nor had I the least desire to taste anything. I now wished for the last friend, death, to relieve me; but soon, to my grief, two of the white men offered me eatables, and on my refusing to eat, one of them held

*Slaves were chained together and then put into the hold of the slave ship.*

me fast by the hands and laid me across I think the windlass, and tied my feet while the other flogged me severely."

An estimated 15 to 20 percent of the slaves died on a typical trip, mostly from disease. Some killed themselves by jumping overboard rather than face a lifetime of slavery. Eventually, Equiano reached the island of Barbados, where he was sold and taken to North America to work on a plantation.

# A Dangerous Place to Live

As the colony grew, the settlers faced threats from the Spanish and French, from local Indians, and even from pirates. In order to defend themselves, the colonists formed a militia, or citizen's army. Every able-bodied man in the colony was required to serve in the militia. When the colonists were attacked, they grabbed their muskets and fought. Often, slaves were pressed into service and forced to fight alongside their white masters.

Wars in Europe among the English, French, and Spanish spilled over into the colony. Spanish and French troops threatened Carolina farmers and tried to drive them from their homes. The settlers retaliated by launching an attack on a Spanish town in Florida. Then, Spanish and French ships attacked Charles Town in 1706. They landed troops and planned to storm the city. The militia was called out and soon defeated the invaders in one of the first victories for the Carolina militia. Seventy years later, the same militia would fight against English troops in the Revolutionary War.

# The Yamasee War

In addition to warring European powers, the settlers often faced threats from local Indians. As more and more settlers came to Carolina, they claimed lands occupied by Indian tribes. Settlers and Indians often clashed over who owned the land. One bloody confrontation, called the Yamasee War, started in 1715. In the next two years, hundreds of settlers and Indians would die and Charles Town would nearly starve.

The Yamasee lived near Port Royal in the southern part of Carolina. When the first settlers arrived in the area, the Indians traded deer skins with the colonists for manufactured goods such as metal tools, cooking utensils, and guns. The settlers cleared land and built farms. Both groups got along well with each other for about ten years.

As the settlers expanded their farms, the Indians feared that the colonists would take all their land. Colonists and Yamasee clashed more and more often. Finally, a group of colonists took some Yamasee prisoners and sold them as slaves. The Indians fought back.

The Yamasee fought back by killing cattle that belonged to some farmers. Then, the Indians struck several farms and killed the colonists. More farms were attacked and almost 100 settlers were killed. Fear quickly spread through the colony. Farmers left their homes and fled to Charles Town, where they demanded that the assembly call out the militia to fight the Indians.

As the war raged on, more and more farmers fled, abandoning their crops. After a year of fighting, Charles Town began to run short of food. As one resident put it,

*"We are ready to eat up one another for want of provisions, and what we can get is very bad."*

The colonists were desperate. They knew they could not defeate the Yamasee alone. Finally, they turned to the Cherokee for help. This powerful tribe wanted to drive the Yamasee from the region. Together, the militia and Cherokee warriors overpowered the Yamasee and destroyed most of the tribe.

Many of Carolina's colonists were so terrified by the Yamasee War that they did not return to their farms. Some areas of the backcountry were not resettled for almost ten years. Overall, colonists trusted Indians much less than they did before the war.

# The Pirate Threat

In addition to dealing with the Indians, French, and Spanish, Carolina settlers also had to cope with pirates. During the seventeenth century, pirates, or buccaneers, operated from the islands of Hispaniola and Tortuga in the Caribbean Sea. They attacked Spanish treasure ships bringing gold and silver from South and Central America to Spain. They also preyed on English ships going to and from Carolina. Spain and England sent powerful warships to the Caribbean to stop the pirates. They attacked the pirate ships and drove them north. Some of the buccaneers hid among the islands off the Carolina coast.

One of these pirates was known as Blackbeard. In the spring of 1718, his fleet hovered outside Charles Town harbor and attacked ships entering and leaving the city. In addition to robbing ships, Blackbeard captured rich Englishmen and held them for ransom. One morning, Blackbeard's flagship, *Queen Anne's Revenge*, led his fleet into Charles Town harbor.

## Buccaneers

The word *buccaneer* comes from a type of food eaten by the pirates. The pirates hunted wild cattle and pigs on Hispaniola, cut the meat into long slices, then grilled and dried it so the meat would be preserved on board ship. The meat was called *bukan* by the local Indians, and the pirates began calling themselves buccaneers.

*The fighting was often intense when pirates boarded a ship.*

The pirate had over 300 men and his ships had many heavy cannons. The people of the city braced for the worst. But instead of demanding gold or silver, the pirate offered to release all his captives in exchange for medical supplies.

No one knows for certain why he wanted the medicine. Blackbeard's men may have been ill or injured or he may have been sick himself. The governor wisely handed over the medicine and Blackbeard sailed out of the harbor without firing a shot. That same year, Blackbeard and the other pirates who plundered the Carolina coast were captured or killed and the pirate threat to the colony ended.

# A Change in Government

During all these battles, the Carolina settlers had received very little help from the proprietors. The colonists lacked the money to provide enough weapons or soldiers to protect their colony. There was only one solution. The assembly sent a delegation to England. They asked the king to take control of Carolina and make it a royal colony. This would take power away from the proprietors and make the king himself responsible for protecting the colonists. To everyone's surprise, the king agreed. But it took more than ten years to settle all the details and for the proprietors and king to agree on exactly how Carolina would be governed. Finally, in 1729, Carolina was split in two. North Carolina remained under the control of the proprietors. South Carolina, which included Charles Town, became a royal English colony.

During the first decades of the eighteenth century, South Carolina had grown from a wilderness outpost into a prosperous English colony. Charles Town harbor bustled with ships carrying goods to and from English ports. New houses and businesses were being built almost daily. More and more settlers moved into the backcountry. The rice and indigo plantations surrounding Charles Town brought wealth to their owners. However, these good times had a price. More than half of the colony's population were slaves with few rights and little hope for a better life. As the colony continued to grow, the huge gap between its wealthy citizens and those living in slavery would shape its future.

## Pirate Aid

Although they were thieves and killers, the pirates helped the Carolina settlers in one way. The colonists were supposed to buy all their manufactured goods from England. English merchants often charged high prices for these products. However, the pirates acquired many manufactured items from the English ships they attacked. They sold these goods to the Carolina settlers at lower prices than the English merchants.

# CHAPTER FOUR
# Slaves and Masters

## South Carolina's Gentry

During the eighteenth century, most non-Indian people in South Carolina fell into one of three social and economic groups. They were the gentry (wealthy plantation owners and merchants), the yeomen (small farmers and tradesmen), and the slaves. The three groups led very different lives. The interactions of these three groups, especially between the gentry and the slaves, would shape the colony's destiny for more than 150 years.

The South Carolina gentry were wealthy farmers and merchants. More than the settlers of any other colony, they copied the customs, dress, and habits of rich English citizens. They read British publications and sent their sons and daughters to England to be educated. They even imitated the British custom of serving afternoon tea.

*A rich plantation owner visits the poor quarters where his slaves are forced to live.*

Many plantation owners built beautiful homes on their estates. In addition, they had fancy second homes in Charles Town. These were made of brick and coated with a colorful plaster called stucco. The planters could afford to decorate their homes with large dining room tables, finely carved chairs, and beautiful paintings imported from England. They dressed in the most fashionable clothes imported from London. They also gave elaborate parties at their houses to entertain their friends.

*Charles Town's wealthy plantation owners and merchants enjoyed fancy parties with music and dancing.*

As South Carolina's economy grew, more and more luxury goods were produced in the colony. Charles Town boasted expert cabinetmakers and upholsterers who created beautiful furniture. Goldsmiths and silversmiths produced fine serving trays and candlesticks. Jewelers made rings with precious stones such as diamonds, rubies, and emeralds. Local tailors produced clothing and wigs for both men and women. These new industries were supported by the vast wealth of South Carolina's rice and indigo plantations.

# The Social Life

By 1750, Charles Town had become one of the wealthiest cities in North America and the social and cultural center of South Carolina. Plantation owners regularly spent part of each year in the city. Frequently, they were trying to escape the diseases that regularly broke out on the plantations. Because rice plantations were often located near swampy areas, they became the breeding grounds for mosquitoes that carried malaria and yellow fever.

The wealthy women of Charles Town entertained their friends at social gatherings in their elaborate homes. They showed off the latest London fashions, which featured lace collars, fancy embroidery, and full skirts. Entertainment included concerts, card games, and lavish meals prepared by a host of slaves and servants.

Dressed in their finest clothes, the gentry attended plays and concerts. The Dock Street Theater, built in 1736, was one of the first theaters in North America. The aristocrats also attended horse races and raised thoroughbred horses. Betting on the races was very popular among the Charles Town gentry, who sometimes won or lost large sums of money on a single race.

The wealthy men of Charles Town usually belonged to clubs. These private clubs, for men only, were modeled after clubs in England. Many men spent part of each day at the clubs, meeting friends, discussing business, and reading the local newspapers.

## Free Schools

The right education was a mark of distinction for the children of the wealthy in South Carolina. The free schools were boarding schools, and many students came to Charles Town from the plantations to attend them. Getting to school could be hazardous. For example, one young man drowned in the Ashley River on his way back to school in 1737.

Boys studied algebra, geometry, surveying, navigation, astronomy, and bookkeeping. Education for girls emphasized polite conversation about "Opera...Stage Plays... Romances, and Other books." One schoolmistress advertised that she taught "different branches of polite education...reading, writing, English, French...music, and dancing."

Charles Town's elite believed that one way to demonstrate their wealth was to send their children to the best schools. These were called "free schools," although those who could afford to pay tuition were expected to do so. However, scholarships were available for less well-to-do children. Both boys and girls could attend school. In addition, many wealthy families hired tutors for their children. Many young men went to England to complete their education.

## Slave Society

While members of the gentry enjoyed their wealth, slaves toiled to make this lifestyle possible. South Carolina had the largest slave population of the thirteen colonies. In 1700 there were about 3,000 slaves in South Carolina. Just fifty years later, the number of slaves was almost 40,000. The lives of South Carolina's slaves were almost the exact opposite of the gentry's. Slaves had almost no rights and lived in poverty. They were considered property and could be bought and sold by the masters.

Slaves were forced to do whatever their masters chose. The masters decided whom and when a slave married. They decided what work a slave did. They decided what religion slaves were allowed to practice. And they decided whether slave families stayed together or were torn apart. If slave owners lost money at the horse races or did not get top dollar for their indigo crop, they might sell off some of their slaves to make up for the losses. Many owners did not hesitate to sell a male slave, separating him from his wife and children.

To ensure that slaves would not escape, the colony passed a series of laws, called slave codes. These laws governed the lives of slaves. Slaves were required to carry a written pass if they left the plantation. They could be whipped and otherwise severely punished if they ran away. Most importantly, the slave codes stated that slaves remained slaves for life and that the children of slave women were also slaves. The only way a slave could become free was to be granted freedom by his or her owner.

Some slaves lived in Charles Town, as servants in the homes of their wealthy masters. They worked as cooks, washerwomen, and coachmen. Others were owned by well-to-do shipbuilders, for whom they worked as carpenters and sailmakers. Other slaves worked for butchers, barbers, and bakers. However, the majority of slaves lived outside Charles Town on large rice and indigo plantations.

## Slaves' Lives

While plantation owners lived in large, richly furnished homes, they built small, crude cabins for their slaves called slave quarters. These cabins usually consisted of one room with a fireplace. They had very simple wooden furniture.

Benches were often made of split logs. Tables were rough planks nailed together. Many slaves slept on straw mats on the floor instead of beds. The floor was usually packed earth covered with straw. The windows were protected by wooden shutters that could be closed in the winter to keep out the cold. However, the cabins were still very drafty and there was little light. In the summer, slave quarters were stifling.

*Slaves lived in crude houses called slave quarters.*

Plantation work was supervised by white overseers who assigned tasks to the slaves. These tasks were managed by black slave drivers who made sure that the slaves completed them. Masters and overseers often selected slave drivers according to the drivers' leadership ability and experience with plantation work. Overseers and slave drivers were responsible for getting the plantation's work done. They often pushed the slaves to do more by using punishment and cruelty. Overseers did not hesitate to whip slaves repeatedly, chain them, and even shoot them. The slaves had little choice but to accept this treatment and do whatever their bosses told them.

## Slave Driver

The term "slave driver" is used today to describe someone who pushes people to work hard.

# Treatment of Slaves

Once their plantation work was completed each day, some slaves were allowed to work for themselves. This included planting their own gardens or fishing to add to the food they received from their masters. This work, which was done after many hours in the fields, was like having a second job. When their masters could not keep slaves constantly busy, they often rented the slaves out to others who needed them. Slaves who were skilled as carpenters might go to neighboring plantations to build houses and stables. Women who were experienced midwives were often sent to other plantations to deliver babies. Slaves were sometimes permitted to keep part of these earnings for themselves. With this money, some slaves bought fancy clothes, others could afford to rent rooms outside of their masters' homes, and a few even saved enough to purchase freedom for themselves and their families.

Slave owners believed they were better than their African slaves. They thought it only natural that they should control slaves' lives. Because they felt they were superior, many slave owners felt a genuine responsibility for the health and well-being of their slaves. They believed they must provide them with food, clothing, shelter, and medical care when the slaves became sick. In part, the owners were simply protecting their investments. The cost of purchasing a slave was hundreds of dollars. Masters wanted to keep their slaves as healthy as possible so they could continue working.

There were limits, however, to the masters' caring. Slaves were expected to do their work and always show respect for their masters. Slaves who spoke out of turn or did not show the proper respect were punished. The slave codes protected the slave owners, who were permitted to use any form of punishment they felt necessary. If a slave was killed while being whipped, a plantation owner faced little or no punishment.

*Slaves were often whipped as punishment. Sometimes another slave who had been made a slave driver did the whipping.*

Many South Carolina slaves died young. An estimated two out of every three slaves born on South Carolina plantations died before reaching the age of sixteen. The death rate for slaves in South Carolina was higher than in other colonies. The intense and often backbreaking labor required to cultivate rice and indigo was one cause. In addition, rice plantations were located in wet, swampy areas. The disease-carrying mosquitoes that drove plantation owners to Charles Town took the lives of many slaves.

In spite of the dangers, many slaves resisted their masters' control. For example, after slaves were purchased, the owners gave them new names. These were often ancient Roman names, like Pompey and Hannibal, or names from the Bible. Unknown to their masters, slaves often kept the names they had been given in Africa, using these names among themselves in the slave quarters. The plantation owners tried to instill Christianity into the lives of the slaves, too. But many slaves refused to adopt Christianity and continued to practice the religious beliefs they had learned in Africa. Many believed that spirits lived in mountains and caves. Some slaves prayed to these spirits to help their children stay healthy, to provide them with enough to eat, and to help them endure the cruelties of slavery.

Some slaves escaped from their plantations. These fugitives headed for the frontier settlements of the backcountry where few farmers owned slaves. A few slaves traveled south to the Spanish settlement of St. Augustine in Florida. There they were given their freedom. A small number of slaves revolted against their masters. In 1739, a slave revolt stunned the entire colony of South Carolina. This uprising would lead to changes in the slave code that would make slaves' lives even worse.

# The Stono Rebellion

On Sunday, September 9, while many colonists were attending church, a small group of runaway slaves gathered near the Stono River outside of Charles Town. Led by a slave named Jemmy, they went to a nearby store, stole guns and ammunition, and killed the shop owners. Then the slaves continued to nearby houses and killed the people inside.

More slaves joined the small army as it moved south. They killed any whites they encountered. Lieutenant Governor William Bull unexpectedly ran into the runaway slaves. "I was returning from Granville County with four Gentlemen," Bull wrote, "and met these Rebels at eleven o'clock in the forenoon and fortunately [saw] the approaching danger [in] time enough to avoid it." Bull called out the militia, who pursued the slaves.

The South Carolina militia caught up with them near the Edisto River. A fierce gun battle broke out. Thirty slaves were killed. The others escaped but were later captured and hanged.

The Stono Rebellion sent a shudder through South Carolina. Settlers lived in fear that another slave revolt might happen at any time. By 1739, slaves outnumbered whites in South Carolina by almost two to one. There were 39,000 slaves and 20,000 white colonists. The South Carolina assembly quickly passed new, harsher laws regarding slaves. Slaves were no longer permitted to grow their own food or earn money that might be used to pay for weapons. They could no longer gather together in groups, where they might talk about rebellion. They were no longer allowed to learn to read and write, since these skills allowed them to communicate with each other. Finally, the slave trade in South Carolina was stopped for the next ten years, because the settlers were convinced that the Stono Rebellion had been caused by newly arrived slaves. The new slave codes widened the immense gap that already existed between slave owners and slaves.

## Runaway Notices

Slave owners who were trying to capture escaped slaves placed advertisements in newspapers. These advertisements reveal that many runaway slaves were skilled workers such as carpenters, coopers, bricklayers, and blacksmiths. Slave owners usually offered a reward for the return of the runaway. Professional slave hunters tracked and captured runaways even when they fled to non-slave northern states.

RUN away, the 23d of this Inftant *January,* from *Silas Crifpin* of *Burlington,* Taylor, a Servant Man named *Jofeph Morris,* by Trade a Taylor, aged about 22 Years, of a middle Stature, fwarthy Complexion, light gray Eyes, his Hair clipp'd off, mark'd with a large pit of the Small Pox on one Cheek near his Eye, had on when he went away a good Felt Hat, a yellowifh Drugget Coat with Pleits behind, an old Ozenbrigs Veft, two Ozenbrigs Shirts, a pair of Leather Breeches handfomely worm'd and flower'd up the Knees, yarn Stockings and good round toe'd Shoes Took with him a large pair of Sheers crack'd in one of the Bows, & mark'd with the Word [*Savoy*]. Whoever takes up the faid Servant, and fecures him fo that his Mafter may have him again, fhall have *Three Pounds* Reward befides reafonable Charges, paid by me *Silas Crifpin.*

*This newspaper ad gives a detailed description of a runaway slave. The reward of three pounds for his return would be equal to about $50.00 today.*

The colonial kitchen was often the center of the house. Whether fancy or plain, this is where people gathered to talk, keep warm by the fire, and of course cook and eat their meals. Colonial cooks used many of the same tools we see in kitchens today.

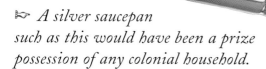

☞ *A silver saucepan such as this would have been a prize possession of any colonial household.*

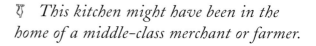

🖒 *This kitchen might have been in the home of a middle-class merchant or farmer.*

♨ *Butchering a pig, as shown above, was often timed for a special occasion. It provided fresh meat for a few days and lots of work to preserve the rest by salting, smoking, and making sausage.*

# Cooking

◁ Three-legged pans like this one were sometimes called spiders. The legs kept the bottom of the pan above the fire.

◁ Common tools found in most colonial kitchens included a mortar and pestle for grinding, a screen for sifting flour, a wooden bowl, a clay cup, and a gourd ladle.

✎ This formal dining room would have been found in the home of a well-to-do merchant or plantation owner.

◁ Pastries were filled with leftovers for supper or fruits for dessert.

◁ Wooden spoons were common in colonial kitchens. The design has not changed much even today.

☞ In summer, cooking was often done outdoors over an open fire. This was much cooler than cooking in a small, hot kitchen.

65

# CHAPTER FIVE

# Expanding Horizons

## Into the Backcountry

At the beginning of the 1700s, almost the entire non-Indian population of South Carolina lived near the Atlantic coast. Charles Town and the plantations surrounding it were located on a flat coastal plain that bordered the Atlantic Ocean. Moving west, the country rose into foothills and mountains called the backcountry. There were few roads and fewer outposts in the backcountry. But small farmers and merchants saw new opportunities there. They began settling the land west of the large plantations surrounding Charles Town.

The British wanted settlers to move into the backcountry to expand the colony. They knew that many people in Europe wanted to come to America to seek a better life.

*A backcountry farm prepares for the corn harvest in the fall.*

So, in the 1730s, the British offered fifty-acre farms to anyone who would move to the South Carolina backcountry and settle there. This offer was taken up by small farmers and artisans from many countries. Among them were Swiss, Germans, Dutch, and Scot-Irish (people from Scotland who had settled in Ireland). The new settlers established their own towns throughout the backcountry. Until this time, most South Carolina settlers had been English.

As these new groups moved into the colony, they brought new religions and social customs with them. They had a different heritage than the English settlers and spoke different languages. This made them less connected to the English traditions of South Carolina's government. Backcountry farmers valued their independence. Generally, they felt less loyalty to the government in Charles Town than South Carolinians who lived in and around the city. Their independent nature would prove important in the years to come.

## Backcountry Life

Whatever their background, most backcountry settlers were farmers. They cleared the land and planted a variety of crops, including corn and wheat. Most backcountry farms were tended by one family of settlers, who grew only enough to feed themselves. Few owned slaves. They made their own clothes from fabric they spun from flax or cotton, which they grew themselves. They often had small vegetable gardens tended by the women and girls of the farm. The men and boys hunted deer and other animals for food and used the skins to make clothing. In many ways, their lives were similar to those of the Indians, such as the Cherokee, who lived in the same region.

## Backcountry Roads

Traveling through South Carolina's backcountry was a challenge, even in good weather. Most backcountry settlers walked from one place to another. Horses were expensive and many settlers could not afford them.

Some settlers used carts pulled by horses, donkeys, or oxen to haul their possessions and travel to market. As more towns and villages sprang up, a system of roads connected them. Colonial roads were not paved. Many were simply rutted tracks barely wide enough for a horse-drawn wagon. The tracks flooded when it rained and sometimes froze at higher elevations in the winter. The roads were used by everyone—settlers driving cattle to market, traders with wagons filled with goods, and travelers on foot.

There were few inns in the backcountry or other places to find food and lodging on long journeys. Travelers looked for friendly farm families willing to share their home or barn for the night. Because travel was difficult and time-consuming in the South Carolina backcountry, most settlers rarely journeyed more than a few miles from home.

*This reproduction shows what the inside of a backcountry home might have looked like.*

Backcountry life was difficult. Settlers had to be self-sufficient. They built small, dirt-floored cottages from trees they cleared to grow their crops. Their houses were furnished with crude, handmade furniture. They worked long hours seven days a week. In many ways, the daily lives of backcountry setters were also similar to those of many slaves. There was one major difference. Settlers controlled their own daily lives and were not treated as property.

As more farmers came to the backcountry, Charles Town merchants set up shops in the small towns and villages.

These stores sold a variety of items, such as ribbon, razors, quill pens, clay pipes, books, women's stockings, and linen and other cloth from Europe. Farmers who could afford them bought these items at the stores. Mills to grind corn and grain were built along the rivers so they could be run by waterpower. Any surplus flour or corn was shipped down the rivers by boat for sale in Charles Town.

# The French and Indian War

In 1754, England and France went to war for control of North America. Because the French were helped by Indian tribes in their territory, the war was called the French and Indian War. Most of the fighting occurred in New York and other northern colonies. No battles were fought in South Carolina, but the war still affected the colony. It brought new settlers who were trying to escape the war into the Carolina backcountry.

France eventually lost the war and also lost its colonies in America. But the war cost England a great deal of money. When it was over, England wanted South Carolina and the other colonies to pay its costs in the form of new taxes. These taxes would ignite the American Revolution. But first, there were other challenges facing Carolina's backcountry settlers.

# Backcountry Fairs

Fairs were held annually in small backcountry towns. The fair was a highlight of the year for many backcountry settlers. They often traveled miles over rough roads to reach the gathering. The fairs gave people from isolated farms a chance to meet friends, catch up on the latest news, and buy and sell goods. In addition to conducting business, people at the fairs also enjoyed shooting contests, dances, raffles, and games.

*People dressed in clothes of the time show what it might have been like to cook in the open at a backcountry fair.*

# Backcountry Justice

One of the major problems confronting the farmers and planters in the backcountry was maintaining law and order. Bands of outlaws roamed the backcountry stealing horses and cattle. Sometimes they crossed over from North Carolina, robbed a farmer, and then escaped across the border. According to one newspaper report, the bandits "have killed Cattle, stole horses, and robbed houses and go armed threatening to kill anything that will [harm] them." Bandits attacked one settler's farm and took everything, including his clothes, bedding, furniture, and farm tools.

The government in Charles Town offered little help or protection. The backcountry settlers decided to take matters into their own hands. During the 1760s, they formed vigilante groups known as the Regulators. (Vigilantes are people who take the law into their own hands instead of relying on the police or other law enforcement officials.) The Regulators rounded up outlaws and hanged some of them. There were no courts or jails in the backcountry and transporting outlaws all the way to the courts in Charles Town was far too difficult. Therefore, the Regulators felt that the only solution was to impose their own form of justice.

In 1767, the Regulators sent a set of demands to the assembly in Charles Town. They wanted the assembly to establish local courts and sheriffs in the backcountry.

In addition, they demanded more representation for the backcountry in the South Carolina assembly. At first, the assembly refused their demands and sent its own band of Moderators to stop the Regulators. A face-off between the Moderators and Regulators occurred in 1769. The assembly feared a backcountry revolt. Finally, the Regulators' demands were met. New courts, jails,

*Lawbreakers were often locked in the stocks. Their head and hands fit through the holes so they could not escape.*

and sheriffs were ordered for some backcountry communities. In addition, backcountry settlers achieved greater representation in the assembly at Charles Town.

The population of the backcountry continued to grow. By the beginning of the American Revolution in 1776, more than half of South Carolina's white population lived in the backcountry. The backcountry settlers did not like many of the laws passed by the assembly in Charles Town. Taxes made them especially angry. They had very little say in South Carolina's government because the Charles Town plantation owners allowed only a few backcountry people in the assembly. As their numbers increased, people of the backcountry demanded more say in the government. They would eventually get their wish when South Carolina joined the other colonies in the Revolutionary War.

# The Great Awakening

Fears of slave uprisings and natural disasters persuaded some people in South Carolina to renew their faith in God. In the mid-1700s, the North American colonies experienced a religious revival called the Great Awakening. Leaders of the movement believed that it did not matter which church people attended. It was only important that they loved God.

Leaders of the Great Awakening, like English clergyman George Whitefield, preached to hundreds of people at churches throughout South Carolina. Whitefield came to North America for the first time in the 1730s and preached in Georgia. He was a moving speaker who won many converts by his powerful sermons. At the time, the Church of England was the official church of South Carolina.

The Great Awakening caused many farmers and poor people to join newly formed Baptist churches. In addition, many slaves converted to Christianity during the Great Awakening. Until then, African slaves had maintained the religious beliefs that they brought from Africa. The Great Awakening resulted in the creation of African-American Christian churches that exist today.

# War with the Cherokee

As more and more settlers moved into the backcountry, clashes with Indians grew more frequent. The settlers were taking over lands that had belonged to Indian tribes for generations. Much of the backcountry belonged to the

Cherokee, the largest and most powerful tribe in South Carolina. In 1759, when farmers invaded the Cherokee hunting grounds in western South Carolina, the Indians responded by raiding several farms. They killed the farmers and took their cattle. Other settlers feared that the violence would continue and they would be driven from their homes. They sent a delegation to Charles Town to urge the government to declare war against the Cherokee. During the fall of 1759, Governor William Lyttleton gathered a force of about 1,200 soldiers and marched westward into Cherokee territory.

*Carolina farmers and Cherokee Indians fight over land and cattle in the Carolina backcountry.*

A poem in the *South Carolina Gazette* proclaimed:

*Tis Lyttleton that doth command.*
*Then come my sons with sword in hand.*
*With him we'll fight, with him we'll stay*
*Over the hills and far away.*

*We'll teach the treacherous Indians how*
*With dire humility to bow.*
*Their savage hearts we will subdue*
*And make them to our King more true.*

Lyttleton's expedition was a disaster. The army slogged through muddy terrain under heavy rains. When the soldiers reached the Cherokee lands, they found a much worse foe than the Cherokee waiting for them. A smallpox epidemic had broken out among the Indians. Soon the disease spread to the colonial troops. Quickly, Lyttleton and the Cherokee reached an agreement. The English agreed to leave with twenty-two Indian hostages. The hostages were locked up at Fort Prince George, in western South Carolina, to guarantee that the Cherokee would keep the peace.

*British troops and Carolina militia battle the Cherokee for Indian lands in western Carolina.*

When the colonial troops retreated to Charles Town, the smallpox went with them. An epidemic broke out and killed several hundred town residents. Meanwhile, the Cherokee attacked Fort Prince George the following February and freed the Indian captives. Then they attacked other settlements throughout the backcountry.

The desperate colonists called for help from England. British troops marched into Cherokee lands and burned Indian villages. The Cherokee struck back and ambushed the English army. "We were suddenly fired upon from all quarters by the Cherokees," reported one soldier. Fierce fighting continued until the British retreated to Charles Town and regrouped. Gathering more reinforcements, the British forces again marched against the Cherokee. They burned Indian towns one after another until the Cherokee agreed to peace terms. The Indians handed over more of their hunting grounds to backcountry settlers. Over the next decade, settlers would push farther and farther westward into the backcountry.

## Hurricane of 1752

In 1752, Charles Town was struck by a major hurricane. The storm began early in the morning of September 15, sweeping away ships, houses, and shops. Some people, unable to leave the city ahead of the rising waters, were drowned. Much of the rice crop for the year was destroyed on the plantations. Exports were cut by more than half. However, the rice harvest was large the following year, as slaves repaired the fields and brought in a new crop. Slave labor also made it possible to rebuild homes and other buildings destroyed by the hurricane.

# CHAPTER SIX

# War and Revolution

## The Coming of Revolution

America was changing rapidly during the middle part of the eighteenth century. South Carolina's population also grew rapidly. In Charles Town alone, the population exploded from 8,000 people in 1760 to 12,000 fifteen years later. Many of the city's residents were struggling to make enough money because the price of rice had gone down. As one prominent merchant, Henry Laurens, put it: "Money is an article that grows scarcer with me than I could have expected."

In the middle of these economic problems, the British government imposed new taxes on its North American colonies. Great Britain had gone deeply into debt to pay for the defense of the colonies during the French and Indian War. In order to pay for all the soldiers, ships, and supplies needed to fight the war, England had borrowed money from

*News of the battles of Lexington and Concord reached Carolina several days after the fighting.*

other countries. Now it had to pay that money back. In addition, England planned to put up a new line of forts on the Carolina frontier. The British Parliament decided that the colonists should pay part of these costs. For the first time in colonial history, the English government imposed a tax directly on the colonists.

The new tax, called the Stamp Act, was passed by Parliament in 1765. This tax required all newspapers, legal documents, publications, and playing cards to have stamps on them. The stamps were similar to postage stamps and had to be purchased from the British government. This meant that the South Carolina courts, for instance, could not operate without paying for the stamps to put on court documents. The stamps also increased the price of newspapers and other reading materials. The colonists were outraged. In Charles Town, a large, angry crowd gathered to protest the Stamp Act. The British, fearing that the stamps would be destroyed by the mob, took the stamps to a fort near Charles Town for safekeeping.

The situation was similar in other colonial cities. Angry mobs attacked tax collectors in Boston and New York City. All thirteen English colonies decided to band together to protest the Stamp Act. They organized a meeting called the Stamp Act Congress in New York City in October 1765. South Carolina and nine other colonies sent delegates. The Stamp Act Congress sent a petition to the king of England asking him to repeal, or end, the tax. The delegates demanded the same rights as other English citizens. They refused to be taxed without being represented in the British Parliament. "No taxation without representation!" became their battle cry.

*British tax collectors were attacked by angry mobs in Charles Town.*

*Carolina's citizens refused to pay the new British taxes. They made life unpleasant for the tax collectors.*

People back in South Carolina were so angry that they organized a boycott of English goods. This meant that no English products could be bought or sold in South Carolina. Similar boycotts had already begun in other colonies. These acts of defiance by the colonists shocked the English government. But it could do little to stop them. The colonies were too far away and there were not enough English troops in America to control all the colonists. To make matters worse, English merchants, who were being badly hurt by the colonial boycotts, demanded that their government end the Stamp Act. The British Parliament gave in and repealed the tax in 1766.

The conflict between the English Parliament and the colonies was just beginning. Each side believed that it was right and that it should continue to defend its position. Many people in Britain thought that the colonists had gone too far. In America, many colonists felt that they had won a victory and should press for more freedoms. Before the Stamp Act, the British had been content to allow the colonists to govern themselves. Each colony, including South Carolina, made and enforced its own laws. As long as British merchants profited from trade with the colonies, the British Parliament did not interfere. Following the Stamp Act and its repeal, however, the British would attempt to assert more power over the colonists in the form of taxes. The colonists would resist each attempt at control.

## The Sons of Liberty

The Stamp Act made many colonists angry at the British government. They formed a group to protest the new tax. The group was called the Sons of Liberty. Its members thought that many British laws governing the colonies were unjust. Many important people in South Carolina joined the Sons of Liberty. The group met at an old oak tree outside Charles Town. The oak was known as the Liberty Tree. It became a symbol of freedom throughout the colonies.

# The Crisis Continues

In spite of colonial reaction to the Stamp Act, the British still planned to tax the colonies. In 1767, Parliament passed a new set of taxes known as the Townshend duties. These were taxes on imported items such as paint, glass, paper, and tea that were widely used by colonial Americans.

An outcry arose across the colonies. Massachusetts and Virginia led the opposition to the taxes with letters to Parliament. The governor of South Carolina at the time, Charles Montagu, warned the assembly not to support the other colonies. The assembly refused to listen to him. Instead, it sent a letter to Parliament supporting Massachusetts and Virginia. In addition, South Carolina, along with other colonies, refused to import English goods.

As a result, imports were cut almost in half. This hurt English merchants. Again, the English merchants put pressure on Parliament to repeal the Townshend duties in 1770.

# Opposition Grows

Even after two failed attempts, the British did not give up. In 1773, Parliament passed the Tea Act. This act allowed the British East India Company to sell tea in the American colonies more cheaply than colonial merchants. The residents of South Carolina acted quickly to show their anger. A large shipment of tea had arrived in Charles Town Harbor in December 1773. A group of planters and the Sons of Liberty held a meeting and decided that the tea should not be allowed to land. Before they could act, however, the tea was taken off the ships by the royal authorities. Meanwhile, in Boston, the Sons of Liberty in that city dumped a shipment of tea into the harbor. This act of defiance became famous as the Boston Tea Party.

Opposition to Britian continued to grow in South Carolina. A group known as the General Committee, led by Christopher Gadsden, met monthly to decide how the colony should deal with England. The committee exchanged letters with similar committees in other colonies. Members of the General Committee included planters, farmers, merchants, artisans, and lawyers. Slaves and Indians were not represented.

## Rice for Boston

Resentment against the British spread throughout South Carolina and the other colonies. The British took action against the colonists and closed the port of Boston in March 1774 to punish the city for the Boston Tea Party.

Bostonians quickly ran short of food. The General Committee of South Carolina vowed to support the citizens of Boston. It sent a shipment of 200 barrels of rice to help feed them.

Soon, meetings of the General Committee were held to consider further actions against the British. Representatives from Charles Town and the backcountry attended. As a result of these meetings, the General Committee became the governing body of South Carolina. South Carolina's citizens no longer trusted the government set up by the British.

## The First Continental Congress

Meanwhile, a larger meeting of the colonies was held in Philadelphia in September 1774. Delegates to the First Continental Congress came from all the colonies. The colonists knew that they had to work together to resist the British. South Carolina's General Committee sent five representatives: Henry Middleton, John Rutledge, Christopher Gadsden, Thomas Lynch, and Edward Rutledge. Middleton was later elected president of the Continental Congress, the first South Carolinian to hold national office.

The First Continental Congress knew that its greatest strength lay in the combined economic power of the thirteen colonies. The delegates agreed to prevent English goods from being sold in the colonies or colonial products from being exported to Great Britain. Among these products was indigo. This meant that many South Carolina planters would lose money. So that they would not be completely ruined, the Continental Congress agreed to permit rice exports. Nevertheless, the number of imports coming into Charles Town fell almost to zero. This hurt South Carolina's merchants. Many people in and around Charles Town lost their jobs. Others uprooted their families and fled the city for the backcountry.

Away from the city, everyday life did not change very much. Small farmers continued to grow enough to feed their families. Some goods were unavailable, but the people of the backcountry were used to hardships. They continued much as they had before.

*When people left Charles Town, they often set up small farms and built simple houses for their families in the surrounding countryside.*

# New Government

These acts against British rule meant there was no turning back. South Carolina had joined the other colonies in defying British rule. No one in the colony knew how far these measures would go. No one knew the eventual outcome. However, the colonists agreed that they needed a new form of government. An election was held in South Carolina at the end of 1774 to create a Provincial Congress. There were 184 delegates, including many artisans and representatives from the backcountry. Without backcountry support, South Carolinians knew they could not successfully resist the British.

The new government met for the first time in January 1775. The Provincial Congress declared that it no longer recognized the authority of the assembly or the governor set up by the British. This was truly a giant step toward independence from British rule.

# The War Begins

Soon afterward, the first battles of the American Revolution broke out in Massachusetts. On April 19, 1775, British regulars (professional soldiers) and colonial militia clashed at Lexington and Concord. South Carolina

Patriots decided that the time had come to take action. On April 21, they took gunpowder and weapons belonging to the English government that were stored in the State House in Charles Town. The Provincial Congress voted to give as much support as necessary to the colonists in Boston. An agreement signed by the Congress called on its members to "go forth and be ready to sacrifice our lives and fortunes against every foe." The Congress also decided to enlist 1,500 infantry (foot soldiers) to prepare for the defense of the colony.

## Loyalists (Tories) vs. Patriots (Rebels)

When the Declaration of Independence was signed in 1776, many Americans opposed it. Those who supported freedom from England and called themselves Patriots were actually rebels. They were defying the established government. About 120,000 Patriots fought against the British in the Revolutionary War. At the same time, about 55,000 Americans fought for the British.

While most of those living in and around Charles Town sided with the Patriots, South Carolina's colonists were truly divided. Many backcountry settlers, wealthy merchants, and plantation owners sided with the British. Patriots called them Tories. The British called them Loyalists because they stayed loyal to the British government.

*Charles Town's harbor was important to both the British and Patriot causes. Supplies for both sides came into South Carolina through the harbor.*

In May 1775, Christopher Gadsden returned to Philadelphia as a representative of South Carolina to the Second Continental Congress. South Carolina Patriots traveled to other colonies to recruit troops. In Charles Town, Patriot leaders seized Fort Johnson at the entrance to the harbor so no English ships could enter. When British ships tried to sail into the harbor in November, they were fired on by a ship commanded by South Carolina Patriots.

Meanwhile, clashes broke out in the backcountry between Patriots and Loyalists, the settlers who supported the English government. Many backcountry Loyalists believed that they would be governed more fairly by the British Parliament than by the Provincial Congress.

About the same time, Lord William Campbell, the governor of South Carolina, fled Charles Town. He feared imprisonment or worse from the Provincial Congress. Early in 1776, the Provincial Congress adopted a constitution and established a more permanent government for South Carolina. In the new assembly, the backcountry settlers made up about one-third of the representatives. The assembly selected John Rutledge as the new executive of South Carolina. He would be called "President of the Assembly" instead of "governor," a term that the colonists had come to hate. The American Revolution had begun in South Carolina.

# CHAPTER SEVEN

# War Comes to South Carolina

## The First Battle

Early in 1776, Christopher Gadsden hurried home to Charles Town from Philadelphia. He had been serving as a delegate to the Second Continental Congress. The Congress would soon issue a Declaration of Independence for the American states. In the meantime, Gadsden had more urgent business at home. Reports had reached South Carolina that the British were planning an attack on Charles Town. Gadsden returned with the new flag he had designed for South Carolina's Patriot troops. It had a bright yellow background with a gray rattlesnake on it, and underneath were the words, "Don't Tread on Me." Many in Charles Town believed in these words as they prepared the city's defenses.

*Francis Marion was known as the Swamp Fox because he and his men disappeared into the Carolina swamps after raiding British troops.*

Charles Town harbor was defended by two islands. Fort Johnson, on one island, had a partially completed fort built of palmetto logs and mud. Gadsden was put in command of the soldiers there. Colonel William Moultrie commanded the troops at Fort Sullivan on the other island. Its gun platforms bristled with cannons pointing toward the harbor where the British ships would soon appear. This fort was also built of palmetto logs. The trunks of the soft, spongy palmetto trees would be the fort's best defense against British cannons. The Patriots were short on gunpowder and knew they could hold off the British only for a short time. Behind the walls of the two forts, about 400 South Carolina militiamen waited for the British attack.

By June, the Patriots were ready. They did not have to wait long. Twenty English warships sailed into Charles Town harbor and anchored outside the city. They aimed 270 cannons at the two forts. Soon, hundreds of British soldiers swarmed from the ships and landed on a small island north of Fort Sullivan. They waded into the small channel between the two islands in full battle gear. But the troops were soon in water up to their belts. The channel that

 separated the two islands was too deep for the English troops to wade through. They tried crossing in small boats, but Patriot troops from the fort shot them easily. The British army finally gave up and returned to their ships.

Meanwhile the English fleet began to bombard Fort Sullivan with hundreds of cannon balls. When the cannon balls struck the fort, they sank into the mud and soft palmetto logs, doing little damage. The British captain then tried to sail his ships past Fort Sullivan to bombard it from behind. Three of his ships became stuck on a sandbar. The Patriots wasted no time. They repeatedly fired their cannons at the helpless ships. After three weeks of fighting, the British commander finally gave up. Fort Sullivan and Fort Johnson could not be forced to surrender. South Carolina Patriots had won one of the first victories of the American Revolution.

## The War in the South

Over the next two years, most of the fighting in the American Revolution occurred in New York, Pennsylvania, and New Jersey. The British captured the cities of New York and Philadelphia and seemed to be winning the war. But in October 1777, American forces under the command of General Horatio Gates won a stunning victory against the British at Saratoga, in northern New York. Historians have called this American victory the turning point of the war. After this victory, France declared war on its old enemy, Great Britain. The French sent troops, naval forces, guns, and ammunition to help the Americans.

The Americans began to win more victories in the North. This caused the British to rethink their strategy. They decided to launch a massive invasion of the southern states. South Carolina would be the site of many important battles in the war for independence.

## The Battle for Charles Town

Late in 1779, the British mounted another full-scale assault on Charles Town. They had not forgotten their defeat three years earlier. This time the English sent a force of 8,500 men and surrounded the city. The British navy blocked Charles Town harbor, trapping 5,000 Patriot troops inside the city.

Week by week, the British moved closer and closer to Charles Town. They fired cannonballs into the city at very close range. The Patriots sent out small bands of soldiers to attack the British troops, but the British drove them back. Many Patriots died defending the city. Finally the American troops could hold out no longer. They surrendered in the spring of 1780.

Many buildings in Charles Town had been damaged by the British cannons. British troops moved into people's homes and took over public buildings. People who supported the Patriot cause were forced to flee, leaving their homes and businesses behind. Many who stayed were viewed as traitors by the British troops. But not all of

Charles Town's citizens were unhappy with the British victory. There were still many Loyalists living in South Carolina. They welcomed the British army and hoped that its victory would mean an end to the war and a return to British rule.

*Carolina Patriots fought bravely against the British to defend Charles Town.*

## Boston King

Boston King was an escaped slave who joined the Loyalist cause. After the war, he wrote about his experiences in the British army. He fought with the British troops at the Battle of Camden in South Carolina and was a messenger for the British. In one battle, King was captured by a group of Patriot soldiers. They tried to sell him back into slavery but King escaped and made his way back to the British army. He continued to fight against the Patriots until the war ended. King and his wife fled to Nova Scotia, Canada, with many other former slaves after the war.

# Wartime Slavery

South Carolina's slaves hoped that the British victory would mean freedom. Many British citizens thought that slavery was wrong. The British promised to free any slave who joined the Loyalists and fought against the rebels. Some slaves ran away from their masters and joined the British forces. But most slaves remained on their plantations and farms. They were afraid that Patriots would capture and punish them if they left, just as they had before the war began. Also, many British Loyalists were slave owners. The British army did not want to anger these supporters by freeing their slaves. As a result, the British encouraged only the slaves owned by Patriots to run away. For most slaves in Charles Town and other parts of South Carolina, the war only meant greater hardship. It did not bring them freedom.

# Controlling the Backcountry

The British army occupied Charles Town for the next three years, setting up its headquarters there. From there, British troops under the command of General Charles Cornwallis moved inland to take control of the South Carolina backcountry. Cornwallis established a strong base at Camden and sent other battalions of British troops and Loyalist militia to occupy the towns of Cheraw, Ninety-Six, Georgetown, Orangeburg, and also Fort Motte.

The British knew that there were Loyalists in South Carolina's backcountry and hoped that these settlers would join the British fight against the Patriot forces. About one-third of all of South Carolina's white citizens were loyal to the British cause. Most of these Loyalists lived in the backcountry. They had always resented the authority of the assembly in Charles Town. They were afraid that a new American government would be worse than British rule. Mostly, they just wanted to be left to make their own decisions and control their own lives. Some of these Loyalists formed militias and fought with the British. Others helped the British troops by giving them supplies and shelter. The loyalty of these backcountry settlers helped the British as they marched through South Carolina. At the same time, Patriot militia forces battled the English as they tried to take control of the backcountry.

*Carolina militia forces hid in the dense Carolina woods and swamps between battles with the British.*

# A Backcountry Victory

In the summer of 1780, the Continental Congress sent a new commander to the South—Horatio Gates, the victor at Saratoga. Gates decided that the American forces should strike against the main British position at Camden. Gates advanced during the night, hoping to surprise Cornwallis. Unknown to him, the British were advancing toward the American forces at the same time. The two sides collided in the dark on August 15, 1780. As the British fired and charged with their bayonets, the inexperienced militiamen panicked and began to run away. "We have bayonets, too!" one of their leaders shouted. "We can charge! Come on, men! Don't you know what bayonets are for?"

But the militia kept running, leaving the other Patriot soldiers to fight alone. British troops overwhelmed the remaining Patriots. Cornwallis had won the battle of Camden, capturing or killing most of the American army in South Carolina.

## The Tide of Battle Turns

The Patriots did not give up. They gathered more men together and continued to attack the British army. Early in October 1780, a thousand British troops were camped at King's Mountain in western South Carolina. The Patriot militia moved in close to the British and surrounded their camp. Before the British could react, the Patriots charged up the mountain. Both sides fired hundreds of shots with their muskets. Time after time, the British soldiers charged into the Patriot ranks with bayonets. Each time, the Patriot militia kept advancing. Finally, the British commander was shot by a Patriot militiaman. He fell from his horse and was dragged along the ground with one foot in the stirrup. The British tried to surrender, but the Patriots kept shooting at them. Almost the entire British force was killed or captured by the Americans.

*Patriot forces overwhelmed the British at the battle of Cowpens and destroyed almost all the enemy troops.*

# American Victory

Cornwallis retreated deeper into South Carolina after the defeat at King's Mountain. Meanwhile, the American troops there had received a new commanding officer—General Nathanael Greene, one of the war's most brilliant leaders. He had participated in many of the battles in the North and had a strategy for battling Cornwallis.

Greene's forces clashed with the British near the town of Cowpens in mid-January 1781. The Patriots surprised the British and destroyed almost all their troops in just a few moments. Only a few British soldiers escaped.

Over the next few months, Greene forced Cornwallis out of the Carolinas into Virginia. The British general finally stopped near the town of Yorktown on the Virginia coast. This decision would be fatal to the British army. Cornwallis and his army were trapped.

The French fleet had come to the aid of the American cause. It was anchored offshore. French ships bombed the British troops with cannons. At the same time, a combined American and French army attacked the British from the land. Cornwallis had no place to run. He surrendered at Yorktown on October 17, 1781. This ended the last major battle of the American Revolution. The colonies had won the war and gained their independence from Britain.

# The Midnight Ride of Emily Geiger

The American army under General Greene fought the British at the town of Ninety-Six in 1781. The British forced Greene to retreat into the woods. Greene desperately needed to get a message to his superior, General Sumter, nearly 100 miles (160 kilometers) away. The region between Greene and Sumter was filled with British troops.

Greene could spare none of his men to make the dangerous journey. Then, an eighteen-year-old girl came to his rescue. Her name was Emily Geiger. She was an excellent rider and often rode long distances alone. She was known to be resourceful, daring, and self-reliant.

Emily volunteered to carry the message. General Greene agreed. Emily mounted a horse and set off. Within hours, word of her mission leaked to a local British spy. The spy sent his best rider after Emily with orders to capture her.

Emily rode through the night not knowing that she was being pursued. The spy was given fresh horses several times by farmers sympathetic to the British cause. As the night wore on, he slowly closed the gap.

Exhausted, Emily suddenly came upon three British soldiers. The soldiers ordered her to halt and took her to their commander. The commander was suspicious, so he detained Emily in a small room. He sent for a woman to search the girl. Before the woman arrived, Emily pulled the message from her pouch and ate it. She was swallowing the last morsel when the woman arrived. Convinced that Emily was carrying nothing of importance, the commander released her.

Emily sped away on her horse to General Sumter's camp. She arrived at about three in the afternoon and delivered the message, which she had memorized.

# Abandoning Charles Town

British troops remained in Charles Town until December 1782. When the British army fled, many South Carolina Loyalists left with them. They were mainly wealthy planters and merchants. They boarded ships for the Caribbean, Canada, and England.

Slaves living in Charles Town had to make desperate decisions. Many had been granted their freedom by the British. Their white masters would soon return and reclaim them as property. In addition, they faced severe punishment for helping the British. Most slaves were too poor to buy passage on British ships. Some made their way overland to nonslave states and eventually to Canada. Some fled to the country of Sierra Leone in Africa. Others remained in the city to face their fate. In all, more than 10,000 slaves fled Charles Town and Savannah, Georgia, after the war.

As the last British troops sailed from Charles Town, South Carolina faced an uncertain future. The war had ruined the economy. Many people were out of work. Hundreds of South Carolina's citizens had died on the battlefield. There was resentment against those who had supported the British. Many slaves had gotten a taste of freedom and were now forced back into bondage. The war was over, but many social and economic battles lay ahead.

We the People

insure domestic Tranquility, provide for the common defence, promote
and our Posterity, do ordain and establish th. Constitution for the Un

Article. I.

Section. 1. All leg
of Represen

The House of Representatives shall be comp
Qualifications requisite for Electors
Representative who shall
Person shall be an Inhabitant of tha
when elected, be
and direct Taxes shall be
all other Persons.

United

# CHAPTER EIGHT

# South Carolina and the Constitution

## A New Constitution

When the British finally left Charles Town, South Carolina faced many challenges. It had to develop a new state constitution. The old British colonial charter no longer applied in the new United States. South Carolina was part of a new nation and would help make decisions about the form of the federal government. In addition, it had to face social and economic troubles within its borders.

The newly formed United States of America was governed by the Articles of Confederation. This document had been written by the Continental Congress in May 1777. It was intended to keep the states united during the Revolutionary War. But after the war, the new nation

*South Carolina would become the eighth state to ratify the U.S. Constitution.*

needed a new document, a constitution, to lay out the rules for the new government.

The Articles of Confederation had left most power in the hands of the individual states. Many Americans, including most South Carolinians, agreed that the states should retain most of the power over their people. State governments were local and easily controlled by the residents. These Americans mistrusted a strong central government. The central government represented by the British Parliament had tried to limit their freedoms. They did not want this to happen again.

Other Americans believed that a strong national government was necessary for the country to survive. The tug-of-war between those supporting states' rights and those who wanted a strong federal government would shape the new United States Constitution.

The thirteen states met in 1787 to write the new constitution. Most delegates favored a strong federal (national) government. They supported the idea that every voting citizen should have an equal say in the new government. At this time, only white men who owned property could vote. South Carolina and other states with small numbers of voters feared that the larger states in the North would control the government. They wanted each state to have an equal say in the new constitution. The convention bogged down in debate over this issue.

# A Constitutional Compromise

The only solution was a compromise. After almost two months of debate, delegates from Connecticut made a proposal that both groups could accept. There would be a new national legislature, the Congress, divided into two houses or law-making bodies. The House of Representatives would be selected on the basis of population in each state. States with larger populations would have more representatives than states with smaller populations. In the Senate, each state would have two senators no matter what its population.

But this compromise did not end the debate. Northern states wanted only people who could vote counted in a state's population. South Carolina and the other southern slave states had a large number of black slaves who did not vote and who would not be included as part of the state population if only voters were counted. These southern states wanted everyone counted as part of the population. Finally, the delegates agreed that three-fifths of each state's slaves would be counted. This did not mean that these slaves could vote. Nor did counting them give them any rights under the new constitution.

# Slavery and the Constitution

South Carolina insisted on another provision in the Constitution: the institution of slavery had to be protected or South Carolina would not ratify (approve) the Constitution. As Charles Pinckney, a delegate from South Carolina, put it: "[We] can never receive the plan [of the new national government] if it prohibits the slave trade."

Many people in the northern states wanted slavery abolished or severely limited. Religious groups such as the Quakers were mounting strong opposition to slavery on moral grounds. Several states had outlawed slavery in their new state constitutions. This was not true in the South. The economies of the southern states depended on slavery.

Finally, the two sides reached another compromise. They agreed that slaves could be imported into the United States until 1808. After that, no new slaves could be brought into the country. Each state would be free to decide to allow slavery or abolish it.

# Planters vs. Backcountry Settlers

The Constitution was hotly debated within South Carolina. Planters and merchants in Charles Town supported it. However, many backcountry farmers were opposed. The backcountry settlers were afraid that the new government would be ruled by a president who would have complete power just like a king.

In May 1788, the South Carolina ratifying convention met to consider the constitution. By a vote of 149 to 73, South Carolina became the eighth state to approve the new federal government.

A year later South Carolina adopted a new state constitution. The first South Carolina state constitution had required state assembly members to own large amounts of land. This gave wealthy plantation owners most of the power. The new South Carolina constitution gave more power to small farmers, merchants, and artisans.

In 1790, the state assembly made an important change that pleased the backcountry farmers. It moved the state capital from Charleston to the town of Columbia in the center of the state. The town's name came from a poem by a young slave from Massachusetts named Phillis Wheatley.

PHILLIS WHEATLEY (1753?–1784) *was one of the best-known American poets of her time.*

# Hard Times

At the end of the Revolutionary War, in 1783, the name of the city of Charles Town was shortened to Charleston. This symbolized the beginning of a new era in the history of South Carolina. However, there was much rebuilding to be done.

The state was devastated by more than eight years of war. The economy was crippled. Throughout South Carolina, bands of Loyalists and British soldiers had raided and looted Patriot farms. Patriot settlers had fled in the face of this violence. When they returned following the war, their homes were often burned and their possessions stolen. In turn, Patriot militiamen had done the same to Loyalist farms and plantations. The property of many Loyalists was taken and sold. Those who supported the British were persecuted and many left the state following the war.

Goods of every type were in short supply. Prices were high for those products that could be found. Blockades and boycotts had stopped most trade with Europe during the war. Many business owners had borrowed money and were deeply in debt. In addition, the huge costs of the war had plunged the state itself into debt.

For slaves, things had not changed very much. While white citizens debated, slaves toiled in the fields for their masters. Any hopes of freedom faded as daily life in South

Carolina returned to normal. The economy of the state depended upon the labor of slaves. The new U.S. Constitution had not changed this basic fact. While farmers, merchants, and tradesmen looked forward to better times, the majority of South Carolina's people were still slaves.

South Carolina had won its freedom from the English, but the price had been high. It would take several decades for the economy to recover. Nonetheless, South Carolina was a rich land. Its people had overcome many hardships in the past. The economy would improve, but the institution of slavery would divide the population for another seventy years. The state of South Carolina faced many challenges as it joined the new United States of America.

*Slaves continued to work in the fields for their white masters following the war. They would have to wait over eighty years to become free Americans.*

# Recipe
## Hopping John

Although their lives were very different, plantation owners and simple farmers in South Carolina shared one custom. On New Year's Day, they all ate Hopping John. This mixture of black-eyed peas and rice was everyone's favorite. South Carolinians believed that eating black-eyed peas on the first day of the New Year would bring good luck. If children hopped around the table before eating their Hopping John, the family would have even better luck in the coming year.

The recipe for Hopping John has been handed down from colonial times and is still enjoyed by many families today.

### *Modern Version*

*2 cups dried black-eyed peas*
*1/4 pound salt pork*
*1 cup uncooked white rice*
*1/2 teaspoon salt*
*1/8 teaspoon black pepper*

- Rinse the peas in cold water and put them in a large pot that has a lid.
- Cover the peas with water, place the lid on the pot, and set them aside to soak overnight.
- After the peas have soaked, drain them and discard the water.

- Chop up the salt pork into 1/4" cubes.
- Put the pork and peas in the pot.
- Add enough water to just cover the peas and pork.
- Bring the peas and pork to a boil.
- Turn the heat to simmer or low and cover the pot.
- Simmer until the peas are tender — about 30 minutes.
- Boil the rice according to the directions on the package.
- Add the rice, salt, and pepper to peas.
- Simmer the whole mixture for another 15 minutes.

*This activity should be done with adult supervision.*

# Activity

## A Southern Fan

Southern girls and women often carried fans due to the extreme heat in the summer months. These fans were often made of wood sticks, paper, or parchment. Sometimes the fans matched the outfits of their users. The fans often contained paintings of simple settings or scenes from books.

Fans had another purpose. Women often spoke to each other by simply waving their fans in specific directions. Below are some examples of "fan language."

| | |
|---|---|
| *Fan with fast movement* | *Concern* |
| *Hit the palm of the hand* | *Anger* |
| *Place closed fan over lips* | *Not able to talk now* |
| *Fan very slowly over face* | *Flirt* |

### *Directions*

*Poster Board • Ribbon • Paint or crayons Decorative Materials (feathers, flowers, fabric swatches) • Stencils (optional) Hole Punch • Large Paper Clip • Scissors*

- Make a pattern in the shape shown.
- Using the poster board, cut nine pieces to make spokes for your fan.
- Punch two holes in the top of each spoke as shown.
- Punch a third hole at the bottom of each spoke.
- Decorate each spoke by painting or coloring, using the stencils to trace patterns, or applying decorations.
- Weave the ribbon through each hole at the top of each spoke.
- Fasten the spokes together by pressing a paper clip through the hole at the bottom of each spoke.

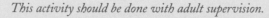

*This activity should be done with adult supervision.*

117

# SOUTH CAROLINA

# Time Line

**1521**
Spanish captain Francisco Gordillo lands in South Carolina.

**1560s**
Spanish build forts in Carolina.

**1663**
Charles II allows English proprietors to settle Carolina.

Captain William Hilton sails to Carolina.

**1670**
English establish first colony in South Carolina.

| 1500 | 1525 | 1550 | | 1650 | 1675 |

**1526**
Spanish leader Vázquez de Ayllón leads expedition to South Carolina but fails to establish a settlement.

**1562**
French establish settlement at Port Royal.

**1666**
Captain Robert Sanford leads expedition to Carolina.

**1680**
South Carolina colony has 1,000 settlers.

Permanent settlement of Charles Town founded.

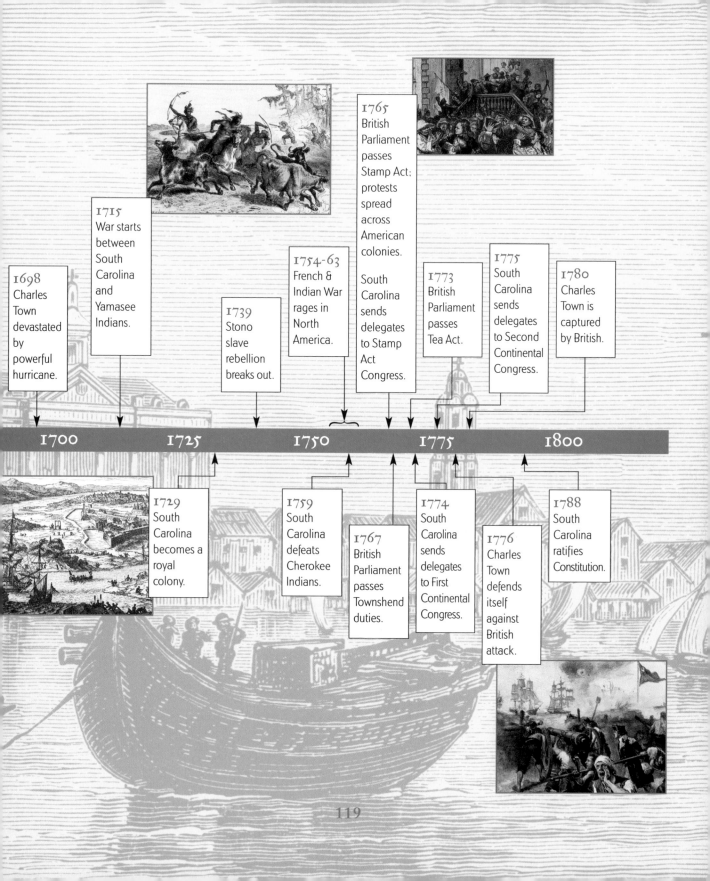

**1698** Charles Town devastated by powerful hurricane.

**1715** War starts between South Carolina and Yamasee Indians.

**1739** Stono slave rebellion breaks out.

**1754-63** French & Indian War rages in North America.

**1765** British Parliament passes Stamp Act; protests spread across American colonies.

South Carolina sends delegates to Stamp Act Congress.

**1773** British Parliament passes Tea Act.

**1775** South Carolina sends delegates to Second Continental Congress.

**1780** Charles Town is captured by British.

1700      1725      1750      1775      1800

**1729** South Carolina becomes a royal colony.

**1759** South Carolina defeats Cherokee Indians.

**1767** British Parliament passes Townshend duties.

**1774** South Carolina sends delegates to First Continental Congress.

**1776** Charles Town defends itself against British attack.

**1788** South Carolina ratifies Constitution.

119

# Further Reading

Girod, Christina. *South Carolina.* San Diego: Lucent Books, 2002.

Hawke, David Freeman. *Everyday Life in Early America.* New York: Harper and Row, 1988.

Marrin, Albert. *The Sea Rovers: Pirates, Privateers, and Buccaneers.* New York: Atheneum, 1984.

Wier, Robert. *Colonial South Carolina: A History.* Millwood, NY: KTO Press, 1983.

Wolf, Stephanie Grauman. *As Various As Their Land: The Everyday Lives of Eighteenth-Century Americans.* New York: HarperCollins, 1993.

# Glossary

**apprentice**  someone who works for another person for a specific amount of time in return for instruction in a trade, an art, or a business

**bayonet**  a short sword attached to the end of a rifle

**cacique**  an American Indian chief in Carolina

**cradleboard**  curved, wooden cradle used by an American Indian woman to carry a baby strapped on her back

**delegate**  a representative to a conference or convention

**epidemic**  an outbreak of a disease that spreads quickly

**flagship**  the ship that carries the commander of a fleet or group of ships

**indigo**  a blue dye used to color clothing

**infantry**  army foot soldiers

**Loyalist**  during the American Revolution, someone who was loyal to the British cause

militia an army made up of ordinary citizens instead of
professional soldiers

overseer white plantation manager who supervised the
work of the slaves

Parliament the national legislature of Great Britain

Patriot in the American Revolution, someone who sided
with the colonists fighting the British

plantation a large farm on which crops are grown

proprietor someone given the right to settle land in North
America and collect rents from settlers

ratify to approve by a formal agreement

repeal to revoke or take back

slave codes the laws governing slaves in the southern
colonies

slave driver generally, a black supervisor who worked for
the overseers and made sure the slaves performed their
assigned tasks

Tory colonist who remained loyal to Great Britain during
the Revolutionary War

tradesman a craftsman engaged in making or selling goods

vigilante someone who undertakes law enforcement
instead of relying on the police or other authority

# Index